Mike Nagler weaves together new insights on innovative leadership in the digital age with compelling stories and experiences that are 100% grounded in the real world. Mike inspires courageous change that scales and sticks because it becomes part of the DNA of how school is done rather than a personality-driven add-on or a passing fad. Mike is a leader who walks the walk and does so shoulder to shoulder with the community he serves.

Joseph South, Chief Learning Officer
International Society for Technology in Education (ISTE)

Mike Nagler is one of the true visionaries who has been leading the modernization of school systems to better serve all learners. This book reflects his insights from deep experience as an award-winning Superintendent and also includes frameworks and guidance to accelerate meaningful improvements. The DEV Leader is a must read for all educational innovators!

Devin Vodicka, Chief Executive Officer
Learner-Centered Collaborative

Students today are wired differently than 20th-century schools were structured for. The workplace and society into which they will enter are experiencing fundamental organizational changes as well. In his book, Michael Nagler has lit the path for school leaders to follow if they hope to address these challenges effectively.

Bill Daggett, Founder - Successful Practices Network,
Founder - International Center for Leadership in Education

Systemic change requires visionary leadership and bold decision-making. It takes envisioning the needed disruption and courageously charting a course to reach levels that previously seemed unattainable. That's the exact type of redesign that has happened in Mineola Public Schools, which has led to increased access, opportunity, and success for all students throughout the district. This book, *The Design Thinking, Entrepreneurial, Visionary Planning Leader: A Practical Guide for Thriving in Ambiguity* provides an evidence-based, experientially-grounded framework for educational leaders to effectively reimagine what is possible for each learner while charting the course, and ultimately, thriving in ambiguity.

Thomas C. Murray, Director of Innovation Future Ready Schools®
Best Selling Author of Learning Transformed and Personal & Authentic

Since the onset of the pandemic, school districts across America have had to adapt to our changing world. Even before that, leaders like Dr. Michael Nagler have had their eyes focused on the change necessary to push innovation for excellence in classrooms, schools, communities, society and beyond.

The process of creating organizations that can thrive in our fast changing world is largely dependent on leadership. The practitioners who contributed to this work are thinkers, change agents and risk-takers. Their thoughtful reflections on the "how to" of innovations and change are a useful guide for educational leaders who are challenged everyday to move forward on ensuring student success in the 21st Century.

Mary Ellen Elia, Former Commissioner of
Education of the State of New York

The
Design Thinking
Entrepreneurial
Visionary Planning
Leader

A Practical Guide for Thriving in Ambiguity

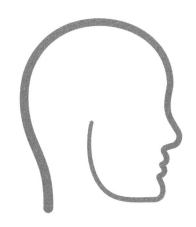

Dr. Michael Nagler

The Design Thinking, Entrepreneurial, Visionary Planning Leader: A Practical Guide for Thriving in Ambiguity

Road to Awesome, LLC.

Dedication

This book is dedicated to Emma and James.
Seeing school through their eyes has inspired me
to be a better leader, teacher and dad.

Acknowledgements

I would like to acknowledge the entire Mineola school community, especially the past and present members of the Board of Education. Change isn't for the faint at heart, what we have accomplished in Mineola is nothing short of a miracle. I have profound gratitude and humility that you have entrusted me with this task for the last 13 years.

Many thanks to the 17 brave souls that contributed a story for the second part of the book. I am grateful you took the time to share our story.

Thanks to Shawn Smith, Kevin Perks, Kim Smith, Mary Ellen Elia, Tom Murray, Devin Vodicka, Joseph South, Bill Daggett, Uncle John Richman, and Matt Gaven for reading and advising along the way.

Thank you to my parents. They raised seven kids who obtained seven Bachelor's degrees, seven Master's degrees and four doctorates. Education is a big deal to the Nagler's.

This book has been a labor of love and wouldn't be possible without the support and encouragement of my wife Dianne.

TABLE OF CONTENTS

PART ONE

INTRODUCTION

Change is inevitable. Over time things change. We have all heard these statements and they make sense. We see it in the life cycle of organisms, the decay of man made structures, and the forces of mother nature - change happens. Every child will grow into an adult, along the way they will change multiple times. Change over time is predictable. It feels safe. When change is predictable it is less likely to garner a visceral reaction. When change is predictable it is less problematic and easier to manage. Change that happens quickly is what throws people off. Sudden change can wreak havoc, like a hurricane, it can be unpredictable and disrupting. Nowadays, change is almost guaranteed. Since the turn of the century, society has witnessed change so fast and unpredictable it has created a heightened sense of ambiguity. It has created uncertainty that pushes us out of our comfort zones triggering uncomfortable feelings of anxiety and fear, leading to risk aversion. The pace of change, especially in technology, continues at breakneck speed. Disruption is occurring in business practices, global competition, and the relationships between man and machine. How do we lead in a world in which we cannot predict what will come next? How do we reframe ambiguity so that those we lead learn to thrive within its inevitability? We must change the narrative from staying safe within the comfort of slow and predictable change to embracing the messiness of not knowing what might come next. We need to *thrive in ambiguity*.

We all need to learn how to confront change and ambiguity since it exists in all walks of society and is pervasive in all occupations. Schools are no exception. Schools are traditional, they invoke nostalgia, glory days, a longing for the simpler time of childhood. Schools don't like change. Over the years there have been countless attempts at school reform, very few of which have been successful. When schools are faced with change, and the ambiguity it brings, they freeze. Frozen in time is not the way to handle ambiguity. Although it is perfectly understandable, it's an emotional response. Like a child that clings to a safety blanket, ambiguity triggers a need to return to normalcy and avoidance of change. Therein lies the challenge. How can we reinvent school organizations to fundamentally change their structures to accept and ultimately embrace ambiguity and change? Enter the DEV leader.

The concept of a DEV leader is a person that combines a variety of mindsets. They thrive in ambiguous situations because they view ambiguity through the lens of a human centered designer - someone who doesn't know the answer to the problem. Their primary tool is empathy - putting themselves in the shoes of the participants. In the quest to solve problems, the DEV leader employs an entrepreneurial mindset. They are not limited to the resources they know, they actively seek to create new ones. These mindsets open up creativity in the organization and, by using the DEV cycle, multiple ideas result in newly discovered solutions. Finally, the DEV leader looks to the future. They paint a picture of what could be. Constantly telling the story of how and why, making people comfortable with the concept of ambiguity - they try to make ambiguity predictable. The DEV leader builds a culture that embraces change like a blanket on a chilly evening. During the process mistakes happen and failure is frequent, but failure occurs without defeat. Change isn't inevitable, it's expected.

CHAPTER 1
PAINT THE PICTURE

People don't buy what you do, they buy why you do it. What you do simply proves what you believe. —*Simon Sinek*

If you're a fan of the Marvel Cinematic Universe you know about Thannos's finger snap - an event that eliminated one third of the population in the universe. It took the Avengers five years to figure out how to reverse the snap and bring everyone back. That five year period in between was known as "the blip." When I think about schools and the pandemic it reminds me of the blip, an almost instantaneous disruption of the world as we knew it and our collective struggle to deal with uncertainty, emotions and new ways of doing things. The sudden, universal change in our lives allowed us to reinvent our normal interactions and radically rethink our professions. Our real life Avengers, the doctors and scientists that created the vaccines, have provided us with the ability to return to normal - but should we? Did anything good happen in education during the blip?

The shift to remote learning forced the widespread adoption of technology and digital resources. One would think that should have happened already, after all we are twenty years into the 21st century, but schools don't readily embrace change. It's a very odd phenomenon, people will welcome the convenience that technology brings in their personal lives but somehow we shouldn't use the same technology in schools. We all routinely ask Alexa, Siri or Google for information yet we still think students should memorize facts. The pandemic really shined a spotlight on this oddity.

I was a convert way before 2020. I grew up with TV shows like Star Trek, The Jetsons, The Six Million Dollar Man and The Bionic Woman. They all depicted a futuristic world in the 21st century; a world full of robots, jet packs, drones, smart watches, tablet computers, communicators, replicators, tractor beams, and voice interface computers. Those shows, in many respects, represented our wildest imaginations. The animators and creative storytellers painted a picture of what *could* be and over time those ideas became a reality, not always fully realized but some pieces were certainly achieved. I wanted to paint a picture of what could be when I became a school leader. When the iPad was invented, I wanted it in my classrooms. As the speed of technology increased, so did its presence in my schools. That wasn't true for every school leader.

Similar to Thannos's snap, the pandemic forced an immediate acceleration in digital learning that was resisted by many for the first two decades of the century. Even though the concept of 21st Century Skills was introduced in 2002, the adoption has been underwhelming (appendix 1). There were many roadblocks that hindered the expansion of digital learning including student connectivity to quality broadband, teacher resistance, lack of an affordable digital curriculum, lack of a learning management system (LMS) that allowed distribution of digital curriculum, and reluctance by teachers to provide live instruction regardless of capability. Probably the single greatest hindrance was parent and community readiness. Without the obvious need, a pandemic, why should we change what wasn't broken?

Not every school and district was in the same boat. Many, like mine, had been working on digital convergence for years. The switch for Mineola public schools was virtually seamless. That doesn't mean we did not have challenges, but the work wasn't new to us. Here is an email from one of our teachers two days after we closed the buildings.

> *I just wanted to say how proud I am to be a part of the Mineola community. Yesterday was an incredible marathon. We had face to face contact with 42 kids. Then, last night, my team set up WebEx parent teacher conferences with 10 parents. They were in awe of how much we've done in such a short period of time.*
>
> *The intent of this email is to say thank you for the leadership you've shown in driving us to be prepared for this. Little did we know it, but we've been training for this moment for years!*

Why were some leaders prepared and some caught so off guard? I believe it boils down to a leader's ability to see the future, not literally of course, but outlining a vision or path for the district that focuses on a changing world. That proactive approach is one of the tenets of a DEV leader.

As we emerge from the pandemic, public education is at a crossroads - the magnitude of which we have never seen. We are in a period of complete ambiguity, not dissimilar to the height of the spread. Two school years have been radically disrupted and we need solutions for how we will bridge the world before the pandemic and the world moving forward. During the pandemic we witnessed a radical new definition of teaching and learning, new terminology: synchronous and asynchronous learning, personalized and blended, remote vs. live, virtual vs. brick and mortar. We need our educational leaders to start thinking like those sci-fi story tellers to envision what a student's world will be like in 25 years, and begin painting the picture of that world. Only then can we begin to prepare them for success in that world. What will that world look like?

FOURTH INDUSTRIAL REVOLUTION

Founder and executive chairman of the World Economic Forum, Klaus Schwab (2016), declared:

> We stand on the brink of a technological revolution that will fundamentally alter the way we live, work, and relate to one another. In its scale, scope, and complexity the transformation will be unlike anything humankind has experienced before. We do not yet know just how it will unfold, but one thing is clear: the response to it must be integrated and comprehensive, involving all stakeholders of the global polity, from the public and private sectors to academia and civil society.

He named this period the Fourth Industrial Revolution (4IR).

To put this in perspective, imagine going to the doctor in the next few years for an injection of nanobots. These tiny robots could monitor our body at the cellular level, and transmit their findings to the cloud for doctors to analyze. Maybe they will seek and destroy cancer cells, repair damaged cells, or deliver precise doses of medicine to infected areas. This isn't science fiction, these experiments are currently being researched and human trials are not far away.

In 1965, Gordon Moore, co-founder of Intel, made a prediction that would set the pace for our modern digital revolution. From careful observation of an emerging trend, Moore extrapolated that computing would dramatically increase in power, and decrease in relative cost, at an exponential pace. The insight, known as Moore's Law, became the golden rule for the electronics industry, and a springboard for innovation. (Intel, 2022)

So what do nanobots and Moore's law have to do with educational leadership? Both are powerful illustrations of a rapidly changing and volatile world of work that we are educating children to enter. We are well into the 4IR and public education is still grappling with the need to change.

We don't have to look far for examples of what Schwab is describing. We have smart houses, driverless cars, digital hotel keys, and some people can summon their car from their phone. We used to call them smartphones, now it's just our cell. We are living in an interconnected world and we are just scratching the surface.

In the big picture the Internet of Things (IoT) will start to collect data about you from a myriad of sources. The most common source will be sensors you interact with and wear (think Apple watch and Fitbit). Data is the Fourth Industrial Revolution's raw material. Companies will pair data with artificial intelligence (AI).

AI is the area of computer science that focuses on machines that learn. Previously, humans had to tell computers what to do. AI focuses on a computer's ability to learn how things are done, then respond to that input. The result is Amazon knowing what you like better than your friends and family. Many people love the convenience of technology without realizing the disruption it may cause, especially in the workforce.

This is why DEV leaders are necessary. Preparing students for a rapidly changing world requires visionary planning. School organizations need to keep pace with the speed of change, particularly when it affects occupations.

Consider the conclusions of the Brookings Institute (Muro, et al., 2019):
> AI could affect work in virtually every occupational group. However, whereas research on automation's robotics and software continues to show that less-educated, lower-wage workers may be most exposed to displacement, the present analysis suggests that better-educated, better-paid workers (along with manufacturing and production workers) will be the most affected by the new AI technologies, with some exceptions.

Jobs that involve judgment, analysis and optimization happen to be the jobs in which AI excels. For example, a radiologist's main job is to interpret medical scans. AI currently assists doctors by scanning a database of similar scans to determine a diagnosis. How long will it take before a computer will do it more accurately than a doctor? The same can be said for professions like chemical engineers, physicists, and administrative law judges. Currently, there are thousands of print news stories written by AI driven software. Many of these news stories are just simple regurgitations of data, like the weather forecast or stock performance. Automation platforms are generating nuanced language, woven into a true narrative that is engaging, friendly, fresh, insightful and... well, human. (Frank, et al., 2017)

The ambiguity around how technology may affect the future of work is unnerving and it can't be avoided, nor should it be. The DEV leader welcomes the conversation and embraces the challenge, always with an empathetic ear. It's kind of like reading tea leaves. The entrepreneurial side of the DEV leader sees opportunities where others do not. We know we are working and living at the beginning of a new industrial revolution. We also know, as we emerge from the pandemic, that we will have new opportunities to embrace different methodology and ideas about teaching and learning. So, how should we proceed?

In 2014, an educational milestone went largely unnoticed. The number of mobile devices eclipsed the number of desktop computers. The computing power in your hand was more prevalent than the box on your desk. On the surface that would appear to be a technology milestone, not an educational one, but consider this - information is ubiquitous and students have all of the answers at their fingertips. The impact of this on teaching and learning is just being realized. Prior to the pandemic, many students did not use mobile devices at school. Virtual learning because of COVID forced the deployment of hundreds of thousands of devices. In fact, the New York City Department of Education purchased over 250,000 iPads with internet connectivity for students during the pandemic. If devices and connectivity are becoming the norm, how can we leverage the ubiquitous information that is readily available?

I believe I found that answer when I attended a lecture by Chris Kutarna, one of the authors of *Age of Discovery: Navigating the Risks and Rewards of Our New Renaissance* (Kutarna & Goldin 2016). He shared his belief that we are on the precipice of a new age of discovery that parallels the period before the Renaissance. Just like the Gutenburg press, the ubiquitous access to information will enable the spread of new ideas and discoveries. How will we reimagine or rediscover what is familiar to us? Kutarna likens educators to the explorers of the past. As we enter into this unknown world, we will be forced to rethink our current maps (methods) and begin to create entirely new ways of navigating pathways (traditions).

As the new Renaissance of education begins, the DEV leader emerges. They become the new "map makers" - leaders that employ skills that are commensurate with the speed of technological change. They paint new maps that guide teachers and learners through uncharted territories and set them on terra firma as they graduate high school. They embrace ambiguity and find ways to make it predictable. They look for opportunities to implement skill-based educational experiences that coincide with what the business world is looking for in prospective employees.

A traditional school leader examines this list and thinks of ways to modify curriculum; they seek to alter the current practice. The DEV leader reads this list and ponders the places that opportunities can be created for these things to exist, flourish, and be recognized. The DEV leader knows that embedding these skills doesn't happen by changing curriculum, it requires a different process, different thinking. It requires educational leaders to use the methods and mindsets of the tech start-ups and software developers, the very people setting the speed of change. If we are trying to create something new, we need to think like designers to find new solutions to problems.

We will find these skills in the makerspace movement, future ready libraries, and project-based learning when we purposefully teach growth mindset and provide innovative learning spaces that align with these skills.

For all of these reasons, we need to look toward the future through a different lens. The pandemic introduced the new realities of synchronous, asynchronous, and blended (hybrid) learning. How are we capitalizing on these practices? The genie is out of the bottle and these learning methods will not simply vanish. We need a shift in how leaders prepare learners for the future. This shift centers on practices that innovative businesses routinely use, namely design thinking and employing an entrepreneurial mindset. The DEV leader is a hybrid, crossing between the traditional norms (pre-pandemic) and a future vision of what school can be (post-pandemic). To find new solutions, DEV leaders think like designers. Empathy is at the forefront of the design stage. To thrive in ambiguity, it is necessary to understand and acknowledge the root causes of the fear and anxiety. Most importantly, DEV leaders welcome failure. They understand that to thrive in ambiguity, failure is common, but it is failure without defeat. Before you can embrace the tenets of a DEV leader, you must benchmark your beginning. What type of leader are you now? Chapter 2 is designed to help you reflect on the answer to this question.

CHAPTER 2
KNOW YOURSELF
AS A LEADER

We do not learn from experience,
we learn from reflecting on experience. —John Dewey

If you are reading this book, you have some interest in becoming a DEV leader, or at least want to understand the characteristics of one. The first step is to reflect on and understand what type of leader you are right now. This isn't always easy to define. Who you are and who you want to be are entirely different things. It's kind of like watching a movie. Movies have an incredible way of drawing us to the characters and leaving indelible memories about fictional people and places. They show us possibilities of who we can become. We root for underdogs like Rocky Balboa, fantasize about being a secret agent like Bond, James Bond, or maybe even a wizard born of muggles like Hermione Granger. The characters may be fantasy, but there is still something about them to which we connect. Their personalities and character traits resonate with us.

Making a connection between movies and leadership can be an interesting activity. If you were being interviewed for a leadership position and were asked what fictional movie character would best describe your leadership style, what would you say?

- Would you name the star character of your favorite movie or would you pause to think about their characteristics first?
- Would you identify with a line the character says that defines how you think?
- Do you aspire to accomplish the same things as the character?
- What is the first characteristic that comes to mind that describes yourself as a leader?

The bottom line is you need to reflect on how and why you do things so you can begin to paint your picture of the future for your school(s).

When I was an undergrad I was fascinated by a political science theorist named James David Barber. In his book, *The Presidential Character: Predicting Performance in the White House* (1972), he theorized you could predict the performance of a president based on his character and personality (summary found in Appendix 2).

Barber used two baselines, active/passive and positive/negative, to create a simple quadrant box in which he can place every president.

ACTIVE POSITIVE	ACTIVE NEGATIVE
PASSIVE POSITIVE	PASSIVE NEGATIVE

The active passive baseline refers to how much energy the man invests in the presidency. The positive negative baseline describes how he feels about what he does. Barber's quadrant is a useful way to examine educational leadership.

To illustrate the characteristics of each quadrant, I associated a movie character to help you visualize the leader. The goal is to place yourself in one of the four leadership types. Be honest with yourself - you cannot improve as a leader without first recognizing your starting point.

THE PASSIVE POSITIVE LEADER: IF IT AIN'T BROKE, DON'T FIX IT

To illustrate this type of leader we are going to examine Frodo Baggins in a scene from the movie *The Fellowship of the Ring* (Jackson, 2001). If you are unfamiliar with this reference, please use the QR code to view this scene in the movie.

One particular scene from the movie describes the moment Frodo volunteered to return the ring to its place of origin to be destroyed. In a group of seasoned warriors and magical folk, a small, seemingly ill prepared leader emerges to accept a task that is doomed to fail. On the surface he was courageous and resilient, two traits that resonate with many people.

Frodo was a reluctant leader. He was thrown into a quest that he did not want or seek. As circumstances continued to unfold around him, he found himself in the unlikely position of ring bearer. He maintained hope and resilience when men, and other creatures, despaired. He longed to return to his homeland, the Shire. What prompted Frodo to volunteer to destroy the ring? Was it a sense of duty? Did he believe he was the only one capable of achieving the task? Did he believe it was his destiny? An answer of yes to any of these questions reveals the passive positive leader.

In the world of education the passive positive emerges as "If it ain't broke, don't fix it." Passive Positive leaders do not view themselves as a change agent. These leaders are wonderful at building relationships and are generally happy in their work, but they believe that if things are going well there is no need to change anything. They are the stereotypical "good guy" whose ascent to a leadership role was primarily based on their relationships.

Barber (1972) describes this type as

> a receptive, compliant, other directed character whose life is a search for affection as a reward for being agreeable and cooperative rather than personally assertive... They are responders, not initiators or pushers, but they go about their work with a different demeanor, and appearance of affectionate hopefulness. They accentuate the positive. They boost. They sympathize.

The if-it-ain't-broke-don't-fix-it-leaders often have the appearance of success in their leadership. The success of the community becomes the success of the leader, which often suppresses individual professional growth and initiative. What emerges is a mindset of just steer the ship and avoid the icebergs.

The passive positive does not see the need for change when others might. The overall appearance of success causes a lack of awareness and empathy. The change initiators in these schools are typically the consumers: parents and students. This is another trait of passive positives, they don't see education as a service industry. There is a void in the notion of personalized learning and there is a general lack of choice for students. If an issue arises it isn't viewed as a possible systemic problem; it's often viewed as an isolated issue for an individual student. A passive positive would think, "Just look at our history of success, it can't be our practice." This attitude manifests into a belief that can cause students to take a back seat because the status quo is the norm.

The Passive Negative Leader: Complain and Comply

To illustrate this type of leader we are going to examine George Bailey from *It's A Wonderful Life* (Capra, 1946). If you are unfamiliar with this reference, please use the QR code to view this scene in the movie.

After the death of his father, George is confronted with a decision to take over the Building and Loan or walk away to pursue his passion. It's the classic movie conflict of wealth and power vs. idealism and virtue. George's loyalty to his family and his willingness to stand up for others are often cited as his more admirable traits.

The happy ending of the movie often clouds the leadership characteristics George displayed. His sense of duty and pride forced him into a profession he did not want. He longed to travel and get away. The scene illustrates his reluctant compliance to take over the Building and Loan, a decision made out of family loyalty rather than desire. His sense of sacrifice and generosity are often highlighted as positive character traits to emulate as a leader, but he was not prepared or passionate about the role he accepted. When things took a turn for the worse, he decided to commit suicide!

Barber (1972) describes this type as a passive negative.

Why is someone who does little in politics and enjoys it less there at all? The answer lies in the passive negative's character - rooted orientation toward doing dutiful service; this compensates for low self-esteem based on a sense of uselessness. Passive negative types are in politics because they think they ought to be... Their tendency is to withdraw, to escape from the conflict and uncertainty of politics by emphasizing vague principles (especially prohibitions) and procedural arrangements. They become guardians of the right and proper way, above the sword politicking of lesser men.

We all know these types of leaders. Their actions and mannerisms are managerial, they are not change agents. I refer to them as "complain and comply" leaders. The most intriguing aspect of this type of leader is how they ascended to a leadership role. How can a leader not want to lead? Consider the cases when long standing assistants are promoted into a larger leadership role because it seemed like the natural progression. Worse yet is the progression of one to a leadership role because it's their turn, as if seniority is somehow a characteristic of a leader.

Passive negatives are quick to point out issues and problems, but instead of looking for solutions, they look to blame. They are the classic definition of a manager and are typically bureaucratic by nature. As such, they like rules and follow those rules, sometimes to their detriment. Take, for example, a new state or federal mandate. Passive negatives will dutifully set on the course to enact the new rule. They will spend hours researching every aspect of the mandate and become an expert on the issue. The implementation becomes less about the reason and more about the process. This is an important distinction, these leaders lose sight of what is important.

Passive negatives will often disagree with the new rule and become resentful that they are forced to comply with it. They make statements like, "No one ever asks the field their opinion before making these ridiculous rules." Negativity becomes pervasive and permeates the organization. Eventually, they comply with the mandate, but the energy and time wasted was their singular focus for an inordinate amount of time. This complain and comply mindset not only wastes a lot of time, it is culturally detrimental to an organization. Since these leaders are quite often very affable leaders with good relationships, their tone sets the milieu of the school or district. They often (unknowingly) create a toxic environment in which people are afraid to take risks. If you did an internet search for "George Bailey, leadership," you would uncover countless articles extolling the great leadership characteristics of George. Examined in isolation, everyone loved George, he was a good person. It is important to note that leadership is often confused with personality, therefore passive negatives can be well respected and admired and still be poor leaders.

THE ACTIVE NEGATIVE LEADER: REBELS WITHOUT A CAUSE

To illustrate this type of leader we are going to examine Roy McAvoy from the movie *Tin Cup* (Shelton, 1996). If you are unfamiliar with this reference, please use the QR code to view this scene in the movie.

Kevin Costner portrays Roy McAvoy, a golf prodigy that failed to live up to his potential. The movie depicts two rival golfers in contention to win the US Open. Roy is a risk-taker, go-big-or-go-home type of player and his nemesis prefers to play it safe. Roy could be described as stubborn and a maverick, but what motivated Roy McAvoy? The scene described places Roy at a pivotal point in his career: make the statistically sound decision or take a gamble, play it safe or go for it. Roy's decisions take you on an emotional roller coaster. At first we cheer on the underdog, hopeful that he wins a major championship. When he drops his second ball you are still hopeful and somewhat proud he decided to forge ahead, after all, he was so close to making it. When he drops the fourth ball, you're angry. His decision making has ruined everything. So much promise and talent wasted. Finally, he makes the shot on his last chance and you are happy again. He stuck to his guns and made the shot only he knew he could make. His self indulgence cost him a victory, future earnings and success, yet he earned a footnote in the history of golf. His attributes in that short period of time include, boldness, self-confidence, stubbornness, doubt, tunnel vision, exhilaration and remorse. These are all traits of the active negative leader making self-reflection difficult.

19

Barber (1972) explains that the active negative's character is

> taken up with his whole performance; he continually seeks confirmation of his self-esteem from other people; in this sense he is highly dependent upon positive response from the environment. He feels confirmed in his expectations by vigorous opposition, but is disconcerted by and strongly threatened by ridicule, contempt, or personal denigration. His tendency overtime is to focus anger on a personal enemy, usually an opponent who he feels treats him with condescension.

The educational active negative leader isn't easy to define. They are enigmas, sometimes viewed as rebels because they do not conform with traditional norms, thereby alienating themselves from colleagues and constituents. They often are very progressive thinkers, but their method of implementation can be haphazard and not strategic. To better define the motivation of this type of leader, I break the active negative into two subgroups.

SUBGROUP 1: KEEPING UP WITH THE JONESES

Unfortunately, public education is a competition. Districts and schools are constantly ranked, sorted and compared to one other. Therefore, schools are often set up to compete with each other. Leaders are constantly bombarded with comparisons to other schools and districts: why don't we have what that school has? The active negative will respond to that question with action. This impulsive, reactionary measure often results in a failed initiative. After all, if your motivation to start an initiative is predicated on having to do it because everyone else is doing it, how successful can it be?

It will be visible when a leader is keeping-up-with-the-Joneses when implementations are "one off" and not part of an instructional model. There will be evidence of a lot of pilots or celebrations of a single innovative teacher's practice. These types of one off practices are often celebrated as if the whole school or district is doing it. Keeping-up-with-the-Joneses mentality often breeds inequity in the organization. Without a systematic plan some children receive a benefit while others do not. This is the reason I despise pilots. By

20

design, a pilot is not a commitment. At best, it's a compromise, at worst it's an appeasement to an interest group, either way it is not systematic. You need scale to have systemic change.

SUBGROUP 2: ROGUE AGENT

The other sub group of active negatives is the rogue agent. As I have stated, motivation plays a key role in active negative decision making. Why they choose to do something is critical to the success or failure of an initiative. The rogue agent is blinded by what they want, not necessarily what the community wants or needs. The leader becomes enamored with a program or curriculum and forges ahead with implementation without support or consensus. They get so self-absorbed they lose sight of the goal.

Both types of active negative leaders are difficult to reflect upon while you are in the job. Unlike the passive leader, this person is doing things. Change is happening, there seems to be a plan, so how do you know if you are this type of leader? The answer lies in scale. Active negatives never see tipping points. There is an appearance of change, but it doesn't take root.

> *I use the word scale a lot. I picked it up from Dr. Shawn Smith, CEO of Modern Teacher and author of The Shape of Change: The Continued Journey of the Digital Convergence Framework (2018). He uses the word scale to refer to a district's success in moving through the seven stages of his Digital Convergence Framework. Digital Convergence calls for adopting new technology, pedagogues, mental models and perceptions about what K-12 education can and should look like.*
>
> *Basically, scale is the percentage of teachers implementing new pedagogy that is current with best practice. When you start an initiative how many teachers do it with fidelity? Smith refers to this as the proficiency tipping point - the period when a leader creates the conditions for something to tip by leveraging the law of a few, ensuring a stickiness factor and setting powerful context for change.*

THE ACTIVE POSITIVE LEADER: DEV LEADER

To illustrate this type of leader we are going to examine Billy Beane from the non-fiction movie *Moneyball* (Apstein, 2019). If you are unfamiliar with this reference, please use the QR code to view this scene in the movie.

The movie depicts the story of Billy Beane, the general manager of the Oakland Athletics baseball team, and the remarkable story of their 2002 season that resulted in a 103-59 season record. Beane has been described as unwavering and not averse to risk, traits that may or may not be beneficial to leaders. Billy Beane changed baseball. He needed to learn new ways to compete with teams from larger baseball markets with more money to spend on players. He made the decision to apply statistical analysis of players when determining a roster. His introduction and subsequent devotion to saber metrics is now a common practice in baseball, virtually eliminating traditional scouts. The discussion among his scouts is a pivotal decision point for this leader. When Beane is confronted by his head scout about challenging the knowledge and intangible metrics that scouts bring to the table, Beane's decision is to try something different. Unlike Roy's decision to attempt a high risk shot instead of laying up in *Tin Cup* (Shelton, 1996), Beane's decision was part of a vision with a plan to lay a new foundation for analyzing data of individual players. There certainly was a risk involved, but Beane calculated that the upside of using data outweighed the traditional reliance on human opinion - regardless of how well informed.

Barber (1972) describes the active positive as a leader that moves from

> decision to decision, he accumulated not just abstractions or information but also judgment, savvy, a feel for the interplay of self and situation. A great deal of such learning is unconscious; the learner may be hard put to tell how he went about it. The active positive person seems to treat his life as a connected series of experiments in commitment.

Active positive educational leaders are obsessed with systems. They understand that change requires the establishment of new policies and practices that ultimately make life (the job) easier. They also know the devil is in the details. The term system can mean many different things. For the DEV leader, design thinking is at the forefront of system planning. Understanding that change is a process and to effectuate change you need constant input, and revision is a hallmark of an active positive. An entrepreneurial mindset is also a characteristic of a DEV leader. You must often look outside of established norms to find the solution that works for you. Billy Beane used saber metrics, rather than the opinions of scouts, to make personnel decisions. That was a radical move. Being the first to try something doesn't scare a DEV leader. Looking outside the professional norms is a common practice.

DEV leaders also know that visionary planning is foundational to the process, they think ahead, but more importantly, they anticipate what the future may hold. DEV leaders try to answer the question, "What do I need to do to prepare my current kindergartners for the world into which they will graduate?"

The fact that mobile devices eclipsed desktop computers is a huge deal. A vast majority of the world is walking around with immediate access to the internet. People routinely "Google" information. Given this fact, shouldn't it be an imperative in schools to teach children how to decipher a legitimate source of information on the internet from a bogus one? Digital literacy is not a formal curriculum and it isn't required by states. Beane's line "adapt or die" is not a common mantra in education, but that doesn't stop the DEV leader. They find a way to embed digital literacy, whether it is required or not. By doing this, the leader is also committing to explaining and defending the reason the decision was made. Cursive writing vs. keyboarding is probably the best example of this. Both have a place in society and education, but which will have more value in 13 years? Answering questions isn't enough - the DEV leader then becomes the chief storyteller.

I like to make videos, it's my primary method of storytelling. I tell stories that capture why we are implementing a new idea or concept. I tweet video clips and encourage district leaders to do the same. The DEV leader uses stories to explain the why. Change isn't a secret. To be successful at change it is incumbent on the leader to explain why the change is needed.

In order to tell stories you need to be present and visible - know people's names, engage in conversation. DEV leaders also look outside the norm to deliver the message. They are active on social media and make videos, write, blog, and tweet. They use the media that the public is comfortable with to get the message across.

> *Perhaps my best story occurred during my first year as a superintendent. I ascended into the position with a split board of education and the hot button topic was closing schools. Two decades before I arrived the district closed a school. The politics around that decision were very polarizing and the school was reopened 10 years later. There was no increase in enrollment. In addition, a new building was erected to house an early childhood center, again with no increased enrollment. We had three elementary buildings housing grades 1-5 with less than 200 students in each. Every conversation before I became superintendent was centered on which school to close. No one ever bothered to explain why closing a school was necessary. I made a presentation to the Board and told the story of buckets, which represented the three major drivers of the budget: salaries, health, and pension costs. The fourth and smallest bucket held the money for everything else we did: sports, utilities, repairs, insurance. Simply put, we couldn't keep trying to pay expenses by taking money out of the small bucket. Any impact on the budget required a reduction of people, which in turn took money out of the other three buckets. It sounds so simplistic, but the Board voted to close two schools. I'll elaborate on this more later.*

Finally, the DEV leader has intestinal fortitude or the act or process of making hard decisions and not ignoring poor performance. Brené Brown's book, *Daring Greatly: How the Courage to Be Vulnerable Transforms the Way We Live, Love, Parent, and Lead* (2015), really highlights how imperative it is for leaders to have difficult conversations. "Regardless of the values you pick, daring leaders who live into their values are never silent about hard things," she says. This is also what Jim Collins refers to in his book *Good to Great and the Social Sectors: A Monograph to Accompany Good to Great* (2006). He states you need to get the "right people on the bus." He writes,

"First, and most important, you can build a pocket of greatness without executive power, in the middle of an organization. . . . Second, you start by focusing on the First Who principle - do whatever you can to get the right people on the bus, the wrong people off the bus, and the right people into the right seats. Tenure poses one set of challenges, volunteers and lack of resources another, but the fact remains: greatness flows first and foremost from having the right people in key seats, not the other way around."

DEV leaders understand the importance of systems but they also understand that they must address the problem of dead weight on the bus. If and when it becomes obvious that a key person isn't in line with your vision and direction, they can't remain in that position. Intestinal fortitude occurs when you begin the process to remove them.

ACTIVE POSITIVE BILLY BEANE DEV LEADER	ACTIVE NEGATIVE ROY MCAVOY REBEL WITHOUT A CAUSE
PASSIVE POSITIVE FRODO BAGGINS IF IT AIN'T BROKE, DON'T FIX IT	PASSIVE NEGATIVE GEORGE BAILEY COMPLAIN AND COMPLY

CAN I BE ALL FOUR?

At a family BBQ one summer, I described my quadrant theory to my nephew, a first year principal in a large urban high school at the time. When I was finished he said, "Depending on the situation, I'm all four of those leaders." While it is true you can display any one of these characteristics in a specific situation, the quadrant is designed to examine your work over time, your tendencies, your personality and how you react to a situation. New leaders may have difficulty identifying with one type and, therefore, should view the quadrant as aspirational. Either way, the talk with my nephew caused me to develop a series of reflective questions to help categorize your leadership style and guide you into the style you would like to consistently represent.

Reflection Question	Type
• Can you identify the "value added" in your schools? • Are you actively pursuing the best pedagogical practice? How do you know? • Have the initiatives you started taken scale? • How do you define personalized learning? How do you measure it? • Are you current in your own professional development (PD)? • Are you overly concerned about failure?	Passive Positive If it ain't broke, don't fix it
• What percentage of your student body do you know by name? • Do you enjoy your work? Even when conflict arises? • Do you spend a majority of your time on managerial tasks? • Can all of your subordinates articulate your vision for the school? • Do you regularly and habitually explain the why to your constituents?	Passive Negative Complain and Comply
• How do you know it's not about you? Do you have evidence? • What motivates your decision making? • Do you feel pressure to keep Up with the Joneses with your neighboring districts? • Do you feel an obligation to please your constituents? • Are you blinded by success or greatness? • Is your legacy more important than the kids?	Active Negative Rebel Without a Cause
• Are you thinking about the world into which your kindergarten students will graduate? • Have you implemented and cultivated systems that sustain your initiatives? • Have you developed a brand that helps you educate your community as to why you are implementing specific strategies? • Do you challenge the status quo and/or current beliefs? • Are you going to where the puck will be? • Do you innovate new ideas?	Active Positive DEV Leader

CHAPTER 3
EnR Thinking:
It's an Evolution, not Revolution

The only human that embraces change
is a baby with a dirty diaper.   —*Unknown*

I started teaching in 1987, four years after *A Nation at Risk: The Imperative for Educational Reform* (1983) was published. The report famously stated, "If an unfriendly foreign power had attempted to impose on America the mediocre educational performance that exists today, we might well have viewed it as an act of war." Over the course of my career there have been many calls for reform that have yielded few, if any, substantial changes. Many cynical veteran teachers will advise newbies not to rush into implementing anything, to wait a few months, it will change again. Truth is, I really can't disagree with that advice. There are too many variables and outside influences on public education to enact broad scale reform.

Over 20 years ago I read a four year study entitled, *The Myth of Educational Reform* (Popkewitz, et al., 1982). Its findings left an indelible mark in my head about how change happens in school and, more importantly, the impact of leadership. The study chronicles the implementation of the Individually Guided Education (IGE) program in six different, "exemplary" elementary schools. Since IGE was a standardized program the hypothesis was that you could measure the effectiveness of IGE across different school settings. The findings revealed that the culture and implementation in each setting were so unique it rendered it impossible to evaluate the program's success. What works in one place doesn't guarantee it will work in another. The study also identified three different types of school culture that also affected the results. The authors labeled schools as either technical, constructive or illusory. These three cultures can easily be aligned with the leadership quadrant in chapter 2. The technical school aligns with passive negative and passive positive, the illusory school with active negative, and constructive the DEV leader. While this seems like common sense, it doesn't deter companies and politicians from asserting that there is a silver bullet to fixing public education.

In *Tinkering Towards Utopia: A Century of School Reform* (1995), Larry Cuban and David Tyack argue that the ahistorical nature of most current reform proposals magnifies defects and understates the difficulty of changing the system. Policy talk has alternated between lamentation and overconfidence. The authors suggest that reformers today need to focus on ways to help teachers improve instruction from the inside out instead of decreeing change by remote control, and that reformers must also keep in mind the democratic purposes that guide public education. Cuban and Tyack conclude that without teacher and parent buy-in school reform efforts are doomed.

Let's look at two recent reform movements: implementation of 21st Century Skills and the Common Core standards (CCS) movement. Although there are many components to the Partnership for 21st Century Skills (P21) Framework, most people define 21st Century Skills as the 4 Cs: creativity, communication, collaboration and critical thinking. Sir Ken Robinson's 2006 TED talk *Do Schools Kill Creativity*, highlighted one of the 4 Cs. Sir Ken challenged the traditional structure and beliefs of American public schools. In particular, he honed in on the hierarchy of subjects in school. He believed school systems around the world are predicated on academic ability rather than celebrating the whole child. His sentiments resonated with people as evidenced by the over 70,000,000 views. His call to action was reforming education to a more personalized approach for students (focusing on passion and interest) and moving away from a one size fits all construct. Fifteen years later we are still discussing this.

Ironically, I believe the 21st Century Skills reform movement wasn't widely adopted because the skills aren't easily measured. So, while we can agree these skills are important, they don't receive the same importance as traditional academic content, which is simpler to assess.

The Common Core standards reform movement, started in 2009, was diametrically opposed to Robinson's call to action. The CCS sought to implement a common set of national standards and assess these standards using similar exams across states. The Common Core was met with a lot of resistance, and as a result, another reform movement was launched, the opt-out movement.

Within a relatively small window of time (2002-2010) we witnessed a reform movement that emphasized skills appropriate for a new century and the adoption of a national set of standards that culminated in high stakes exams. The myth of educational reform strikes again!

What are leaders supposed to do? The juxtaposition of standardized exams and the 4 Cs highlight the difficulty in successfully implementing any initiative.

The entrepreneurial side of the DEV leader kicks in and they ponder how other professions do it. In general, businesses need to respond to change much quicker than schools. Market fluctuation and the convenience of technology have a greater impact on sales and profits, just ask Kodak or Blockbuster, both of which succumbed to rapid change in product use and adoption. Profits and stakeholders require industry to pay more attention and be responsive to technological change. In *Human + Machine: Reimagining Work in the Age of AI* (Daugherty & Wilson, 2018), the authors take a practical approach when addressing artificial intelligence, robots and the implications on the future of work. "Human strengths like creativity, improvisation, dexterity, judging and social and leadership abilities are still relevant and important, as are machine strengths like speed, accuracy, repetition, predictive capabilities and scalability. When businesses recognize the relative strengths of each, they can improve the effectiveness and motivation of their employees at the same time that they can boost their top and bottom lines." They created the concept of the "missing middle," a space where new jobs and careers are created with humans and machines complementing each other rather than competing with each other.

The missing middle

Reprinted with permission of Harvard Business Publishing from Human + Machine: Reimagining Work in the Age of AI by Paul Daugherty H. James Wilson, Harvard Business Review Press, 2018. Copyright 2018 Accenture Global Solutions Limited.

Lead	Empathize	Create	Judge	Train	Explain	Sustain	Amplify	Interact	Embody	Transact	Iterate	Predict	Adapt
				Humans complement machines			AI gives humans superpowers						
Human-only activity				Human and machine hybrid activities						Machine-only activity			

The missing middle diagram demonstrates the bridge between two sides. Instead of viewing it from an either/ or lens (human or machine), the authors develop a space where the two coexist. More importantly he demonstrates how the two can coexist *and* complement each other to make an even stronger link between the two. The DEV leader applies the missing middle concept and builds bridges between the old and the new.

When educational leaders grapple with the challenge of changing school, we see traditional vs. innovative, instead of human vs. machine. Reforms attempt to substitute a new concept or practice as a replacement for traditional norms. This type of change is naturally abrupt and the system reacts. This reminds me of the old adage stating that if you put a frog in boiling water it will jump out. If you place the frog in tepid water and bring it to a boil, you will cook it. Slow change over time works. The missing middle doesn't attempt to replace humans or machines. Instead, it carves out space for them to complement each other. Reform movements don't do this well. They tend to be *revolutionary* and it is too much change for the system to handle. The simple truth is that fast, abrupt change - like a revolution - doesn't happen in public education. When meaningful change does happen, it requires buy-in, and it usually happens slowly over time.

We need to start embracing a new way of thinking. The concept of thinking in terms of evolution, not revolution (EnR) will provide a better mechanism and establish a culture for long-term change.

EnR thinking is the practice of looking for opportunities to plant seeds of the future, then actively cultivating their growth. This thinking plays a prominent role in the DEV cycle that I describe in chapter 4.

There are 4 tenets of EnR thinking:

- Bridging the chasm between what you want to do and what you have to do - fostering creativity in learners while still meeting all of our requirements and mandates.
- Purposeful, incremental change toward a revolutionary idea - paint the picture of a desired outcome and actualize small pieces of a puzzle that eventually creates the picture.
- Creating systems that allow for implementation at scale - the revolution will never occur if only a few teachers are fighting the battle. DEV leaders design, implement and enforce systems that allow full participation of all the players.
- Encouraging and supporting autonomy within the organization - DEV leaders understand that organizations don't need robots. They need individuals who know the desired outcome and work collectively to achieve it.

CANDYLAND

If we spend the majority of our time as leaders reacting to situations and mandates, we will not see the forest for the trees. Leadership's primary goal should be proactive - establishing a pathway forward. As we learned in the last chapter, it's perfectly normal, for a variety of reasons, for leaders to be passive and just steer the ship. However, change does not happen with that mindset. EnR thinking provides a mechanism that allows any type of leader to enact change. It encourages a passive leader to lay out a pathway that is in their comfort zone. Some leaders need to dip their toe in the water while others jump in the deep end. Both are perfectly acceptable as long as you don't drown.

Implementing Mineola's computer science initiative is a good example. Computer science was not a mandated course, there was neither a curriculum nor a state exam. There was no reason to implement the program, but we felt it was an incredibly important topic for students to learn. Once that decision was made we had to calculate how to accomplish the goal (full story in chapter 9). At that point, EnR thinking kicked in kind of like the path in the game Candyland. The pathway twists and turns (sometimes you may go backwards), and the journey is up to you and the other players. Your leadership role and presence will diminish over time as the players move across the board. In Mineola, we established systems, curriculum and professional development opportunities to scale the work. We also created dedicated personnel positions and, over time, it gained momentum and student interest. Computer science did not become a separate class, nor did it replace another subject. We introduced it into established courses and we created independent opportunities for it.

Fast forward five years and *every* ninth grade student in Mineola High School was enrolled in Advanced Placement Computer Science Principles. The students were ready and prepared after years of learning in the younger grades. We accomplished a milestone that was revolutionary, but it took a lot of work and time to achieve. It evolved. The pathway we established was the bridge between what we wanted to do and what we had to do. In this case, there was not a mandate to do anything, instead there was an understanding and commitment to the why, deepening the investment made by all of the leaders that worked on the project. This is why we need DEV leaders.

Now, let's examine how EnR thinking can work when trying to reconcile two apparent opposing forces - creativity (4 Cs) and Common Core standards. Creativity, communication, collaboration and critical thinking, similar to computer science, is not mandated in any curriculum or coursework. While they should be omnipresent in every subject, we don't speak about them, primarily because what gets measured, gets done. Sometimes things that don't get measured do not get attention. The revolutionary implementation of the 4 Cs would be to overhaul every subject and grade level curricula, call out specific instances, opportunities and projects, and embed a "C" in it, similar to the technology competencies of the 1990's. The evolutionary implementation might be to redesign classroom furniture and create more collaborative and innovative spaces. EnR thinking focuses on smaller interventions that can grow rapidly to scale.

In Mineola, we asked for volunteers that would change their lesson design to highlight the 4 Cs in their content areas. If they volunteered, we created a Starbucks classroom for them (see chapter 8). Those pioneering teachers influenced others and the tortoise was off! Of course, teachers could change their teaching practice at any time without new furniture, and we witnessed that as well. Instead of forcing a change that probably would have been met with resistance, EnR thinking sought another way.

The Common Core standards were no different. New York State switched to the Common Core standards and launched a website entitled EngageNY. The website offered free math and English Language Arts modules in line with the new standards - essentially a new curriculum (although they later insisted the modules were not supposed to be adopted as curriculum). In Mineola, we gave each grade level instructional team the choice to adopt the modules as they were or modify as they saw fit. That choice was EnR thinking in action. We knew the CCS would take years to fully implement; there was no advantage in forcing an immediate change in curriculum without allowing teachers the opportunity to test drive it. Moreover, we needed the ability to create a mechanism to assess the standards. Over time, teachers created a robust integrated curriculum and new assessments (more on these in chapters 6 and 7).

The last tenet of EnR thinking, and the most often overlooked, is developing talent within your organization. The idea behind this comes from Bill Belichick, the future Hall of Fame coach of the New England Patriots. He has two mantras for his team: "do your job" and "next man up."

I equate do your job with autonomy. A healthy organization is one in which everyone is on the same page. That does not mean they all write the same way or use the same color, it means we are all working toward a common mission and vision. We need to allow our leaders autonomy in how they get things done, as long as it is in line with the big picture. That does not mean I don't want to know everything, but staying informed and telling people what to do are two very different things.

Belichick's second mantra, next man up, is equally critical. If one person leaves, no matter who they are, the organization must function without interruption. EnR thinking includes personnel. DEV leaders are constantly cultivating a leadership pipeline. This is not limited to prospects within the organization. The entrepreneurial leader is well connected in local organizations and universities, constantly on the lookout for talented people that can help scale the work.

EnR thinking is the most important and versatile tool in the DEV leader's toolbox. It is organic and grassroots, ideas that take shape over time. I often refer to myself as an idea man - I tell the story of what could be, find champions to cultivate the work, and watch the seeds grow. EnR thinking is the precursor to the DEV cycle. Highly intentional steps along the way allow DEV leaders to fully implement a revolutionary idea.

CHAPTER 4
THE DEV CYCLE

A picture is worth a thousand words.
—Unknown

The development, or dev, cycle is a common term used in software development. It describes the structured flow of phases developers follow to build, launch and improve software development and implementation. The cycle creates timelines and prioritizes improvements. While this is a common practice in business, it's not in education - but it should be. In order to implement change at scale, a leader needs to build a culture that creates a cyclical process of ideation, failure, correction, and assessment. More importantly, everyone in the organization needs to understand how the pieces fit. That all begins with a clear, easily understood vision for the future.

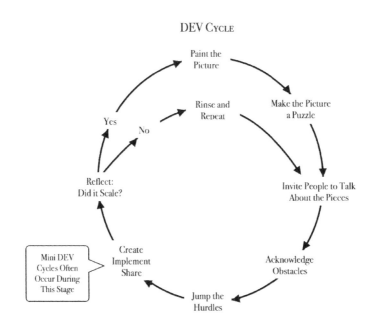

Paint the Picture

Leaders need to easily articulate their vision for a school or district. Sometimes we get so absorbed in the now that we forget that planning is about the future. Introducing a new initiative or program is a multi-year process and the vision for that initiative should focus on three to four years *after* it is started. It is very much like the Wayne Gretzky saying, "I skate to where the puck is going to be, not where it has been." One way to look at it is to focus on your current kindergarten cohort. As they make their way through the grades, what will they experience? Will those experiences match the speed of change in society? When they graduate in 13 years will they be prepared for an ambiguous world?

Consider this: A high school senior in 2020 entered kindergarten in 2007, the same year the iPhone was launched. Within seven years of the launch, the number of mobile devices exceeded desktop computers. How did schools react? For the most part they didn't. Now replace the high school senior with a child beginning kindergarten in 2020. What will schools do to prepare them for their graduation in 2037? It is absolutely critical to educate our communities on the pace of technological change and, more importantly, why schools need to keep up with that speed of change.

You don't need to be Nostradamus to paint this picture. We can make some reasonable conclusions if we postulate.

If we know:

- The proliferation of mobile devices (in life and school) will lead to greater access to information for everyone. The need to remember facts and figures will diminish because they are readily available, therefore the emphasis on teaching and learning content should shift to a more analytical and problem solving skill set.

- Artificial intelligence, robotics and data will continue to grow (almost exponentially) during the upcoming years. As such, computer science, computational thinking and coding are necessary skills that all students should master
- Social media has created the phenomenon of echo chambers (see appendix 3) and isolation. Information literacy and social emotional learning need to be part of a responsible curriculum.

These are three examples of factual and observational happenings in the world and our schools. What are we doing about them?

The purpose of painting the picture is to frame out reasonable observations of current and future realities and ask what we are doing about them. The answers you receive will help establish the building blocks for the next step. Remember that EnR thinking must dominate when you paint your picture. This is NOT the time in the cycle to launch a new coding or social emotional learning (SEL) platform - that would be revolutionary. It is the time to be provocative, pose "what if" scenarios and generally think big. The feedback and reaction from the school community will help shape the picture. Finally, the DEV leader's passion and persuasion is most evident during this stage of the cycle. Please note that persistence is required here: articulating the why and building consensus at this stage will only make the next steps easier.

MAKE THE PICTURE A PUZZLE

In practice, your newly painted picture is really a giant puzzle. The entire picture cannot be painted at once. In order to actualize the vision you need a starting point. Therefore, in reality your picture becomes a puzzle where individuals and groups work collectively to put the pieces together. Think of the saying: "How do you eat an elephant? One bite at a time." There will be hundreds of pieces jumbled together that will eventually coalesce to form your picture. The next challenge is deciding on a starting point. This is usually determined by finding your champions, those people in the organization that are passionate about the topic, and empowering them to start the ball rolling.

The pieces of the puzzle are very much like the concept that start-up companies use called minimum viable product (MVP).

> A minimum viable product is a version of a product with just enough features to be usable by early customers who can then provide feedback for future product development. A focus on releasing an MVP means that developers potentially avoid lengthy and unnecessary work.(Ries, 2017)

Start-up companies need to be nimble and quick to determine if the product they are developing will make money. To do this start-ups often release products before they are 100% ready. They continue to refine and improve the product, often based on negative customer feedback. New versions, updates and releases are common occurrences. This is not a typical strategy in school. Between the ideas, committees, research, and demos it could be a year before a school implements something.

Implementing your puzzle pieces using the MVP concept will accelerate the DEV cycle. Be cautious though, the MVP process requires the launch team to be comfortable with ambiguity. In many respects, they may be building the plane while they are flying it.

Guiding principles for puzzle pieces:
1. Choose a starting point.
   a. Which grade level will give you the greatest impact for a K-12 initiative?
   b. Which staff member will be this initiative's greatest champion?
2. Every student must have access to the initiative.
   a. Look to implement the idea in classes and courses that everyone takes, e.g. library, art, music.
3. Don't use the word "pilot." It implies short term and experimental. Phase 1 is a much better term.
4. Make sure you can support the initiative with time, money and personal attention.

Invite People to Talk About the Pieces

Leaders have a captive audience of highly educated and experienced work force and we don't leverage their collective expertise and knowledge. The most effective way to scale innovation and change is to allow teachers and staff to be the designers, after all they are the implementers. One thing design thinking teaches us is to get a lot of different perspectives around the issue and generate ideas. Ideation is a critical step that many leaders forget. The DEV leader's role is to paint a big picture, they should not care how it's implemented as long as it is implemented with fidelity. Don't micromanage the process! This stage also speaks to one of the tenets of EnR thinking - encouraging and supporting autonomy within the organization.

This is also the stage where you find influencers. This term comes from social media and it references people that help sell a product - one of the pieces of the puzzle. Consider this definition,

> Influencers are thought leaders who generate conversations, drive engagement, and set trends amongst a receptive audience, positioning them well to partner with brands on sponsored content. Influencers can break through the noise of traditional advertising and spread a brand's message to the intended audience in an authentic, natural way. (mediakix, 2019)

Every building and district has unofficial influencers on staff, these are the people that need to be at the table. Moreover, DEV leaders must seek, engage and help cultivate influencers. Let's consider a simple example. Mrs. Johnson is a librarian that is introducing coding to Mrs. Smith's kindergarten class. The students were so excited when they returned from the library that Mrs. Smith went to speak to Mrs. Johnson to find out more. The two teachers collaborated on a classroom activity that extended the coding concept into a series of lessons. When the students went back to the library, Mrs. Johnson was able to dive even deeper into the concept. Both teachers documented the lesson with pictures and posted it on social media using a hashtag the district developed for the coding initiative. Several parents liked and retweeted the pictures. One parent retweeted it with a comment and directed it to a local newspaper. The local newspaper decides to write a story that intrigues a national newspaper.

The national paper contacts the principal to do a follow up story which is highlighted in the weekend edition. Of course, the other kindergarten teachers don't want to be left out and a larger collaboration begins. While this is not an example of an influencer in the traditional sense, it is a process that achieves the same results: scaling your vision and expanding your sphere of influence.

DEV leaders, by default, are influencers. They get people talking, sharing and experimenting, which is the most critical part of the dev cycle.

ACKNOWLEDGE OBSTACLES

It is inevitable that there is going to be a problem in the implementation of the work. Expect it, welcome it. It's OK to make mistakes, in fact, it's encouraged. The naysayers will find multiple reasons why something won't work and the DEV leader must be prepared to acknowledge these obstacles and work to find solutions. Most negativity in school settings revolves around a reluctance to do extra work and lack of awareness or knowledge about the initiative. It's new and it will prompt change, expect people to resist.

Two major strategies during this phase:
1. Commit the resources. Be prepared to spend money appropriately. If you ask teachers to write curriculum or design lessons then you should pay them or give them release time to accomplish this. If the initiative is important, then you should be happy to pay the architects. You also get a much deeper buy-in from the implementers.

2. Everyone must understand WHY the school or district is undertaking this challenge. This is when the storytelling skills of the DEV leader come into play. Sometimes you have to find other ways to describe how and why. I find analogies are particularly effective in explaining difficult or controversial topics. For example, teaching coding to five year olds seems frivolous until you explain how prevalent code is in everyday life. It's hard to find an aspect of modern life that doesn't involve some semblance of code. In addition, coding is another name

for sequencing, which is a foundational skill in kindergarten. Making those connections for teachers and parents will help the implementation scale. It also helps to explain that a five-year old's life will be much different than an adult teacher's life.

Sometimes you have to pivot. After I visited Elizabeth Forward School District, I fell in love with their digital badges for pre-K students. I brought the idea back to Mineola. After we invited people to talk about and outline how this piece fit into the larger picture, we implemented it the next fall. The teachers were on board, but we had a lot of difficulties with the digital format. The technology worked fine, but it was clunky for the teachers and parents. The feedback said it was a great idea, but the frustration around the work of issuing badges and communicating with parents almost killed the project. We knew we couldn't continue the initiative as designed. So, we pivoted. We abandoned the digital structure and moved toward a sticker book concept instead. Most of that work took place in the next stage - Jump the Hurdles.

Jump the Hurdles

DEV leaders realize that change can and will be messy. They also know that failure is necessary to advance innovation. A natural part of the DEV cycle is the ability to jump hurdles. I love the term creative chaos: the process of brainstorming and iterating that leads to innovation. Brainstorming is my favorite part of my job. Working with a group of people, standing in front of a white board with multiple colored markers is exciting to me. Scribbling notes and pictures as people shout out ideas is an invigorating part of the cycle. This should be a common occurrence. Ideation is a fundamental part of design thinking and therefore a foundational tenet of a DEV leader. This is also the phase of the cycle that requires the entrepreneurial mindset - sometimes solutions have to be invented.

Before I became superintendent, we worked on a project to implement standards-based report cards. It was in line with the new Common Core standards and it was a long and tedious process. We had multiple committees and each grade level had its own template with the appropriate anchor and sub standards. Visually, the report cards were impressive and everyone was proud of the work. We rolled out a series of workshops for parents on how to interpret the report card and we launched in the fall. When it came time for teachers to fill out the report cards we were faced with an immense hurdle - no one kept grades by standards. This was a tremendous oversight that no one foresaw. There really wasn't an apparent solution, until circumstance presented itself.

Early in the next semester, I did a favor for a friend and took a meeting with a start-up company that was working with Verizon on iPad applications. After a few minutes into the presentation, I realized the product wasn't for us. However, the premise of the product appeared that it could help with our standards-based report card. I asked if they were willing to make changes to their product. When they replied yes, we spent the next two hours storyboarding a solution to our report card problem. It was an exciting conversation and they promised to have a prototype in a few weeks. When they returned with their new product, School4One (S4O), it was the solution to our problem and accelerated the implementation of a standards-based digital curriculum.

The outcome of that meeting was a 10-year mutually beneficial partnership. They needed a high profile customer and I needed a standards-based LMS that, at the time, didn't exist. We worked together to create, brainstorm and modify the app so it was attractive to many educators. We hosted regional visits so S4O could show off the product in action and my teachers gave testimonials. Two very different entrepreneurs found each other by happenstance and a partnership grew.

Educational leaders often shy away from start-ups because the product is developmental. They purchase canned products that may or may not achieve all of their goals. DEV leaders see possibilities. They know start-ups need to test and retest the product and, in exchange for the "playground," the school has the ability to alter and amend the product when it is in its infancy. They take calculated risks with an eye to the future. They think like the entrepreneurs with whom they partner.

CREATE, IMPLEMENT AND SHARE

As I mentioned during the Acknowledge Obstacles phase, it is inevitable that there will be a problem in the implementation of the work. Expect it, welcome it. It's OK to make mistakes, in fact it's encouraged. This is also true for the Creation and Implementation stage. Many things look good on paper until you use it in class. The first time you run through the DEV cycle everything is a prototype. This is probably true every time you Rinse and Repeat, creating a mini cycle during this phase. As the implementation happens, it is imperative the designers meet and discuss on a regular basis. A DEV cycle within the cycle takes place so modifications and corrections can be made quickly. Remember the idea of a start-up's minimum viable product (MVP) - the implementation should literally be considered a work in progress. As teachers implement lessons or work with a product, they need the ability to discuss and ideate improvements to the prototype. What changes should be made immediately? What new ideas will help the product, but need time to develop? These conversations are critical to scale the work. The more opportunity the architects and implementers have in the design, the greater the buy-in. When teachers see the value of the work and feel part of the ownership, the impact on the organization is greater. The DEV leader finds the time for teachers and designers to meet and discuss during this critical period.

The other critical component of scaling the work is sharing it. This is another piece I find too many leaders omit in an implementation phase. I am of the belief that if you create something you are proud of you should make it available to any interested party. In my mind, it is a method of helping to bring equity to public education. Imagine if every district made all of its resources part of an Open Educational Resource (OER) network.

In addition to OER, leveraging social media is critical. Branding has become a popular method to reach outside your brick and mortar building. This is a very simple and effective way to showcase happenings in your building or district. Additionally, a DEV leader can tailor the message going out. We encourage every employee and parent to use #MineolaProud when using social media. It is a fantastic way for parents to see what is happening in the classroom. Using #MineolaProud does not preclude a kindergarten teacher bragging about a growth mindset lesson to also add #MineolaGrows. One hashtag touts a specific classroom activity that is also a part of a larger district-wide initiative. The sharing is critical to scaling the work. Everyone in the school community should understand and see representations of the puzzle pieces.

REFLECT

Although reflection occurs at every stage of the DEV cycle, there should be a time allocated for a summary review, which usually takes place at the end of the year and spells out next steps. The summer provides a chunk of time to take a deeper dive into curriculum rewrites, additional PD or an exploration of different technology. If the to-do list is extensive the DEV cycle will begin anew in September. Changes that occurred over the summer will require the same steps in the cycle to ensure they were on point and productive. The changes also represent the addition of more puzzle pieces. As an initiative grows, so does the puzzle. Eventually, these pieces will join other pieces to start a completely different DEV cycle. Chapter 10 will provide an example of how Mineola's growth mindset initiative expanded and grew to encompass our Response to Intervention (RTI) model for behavior and culturally responsive curriculum.

RINSE AND REPEAT

The word cycle may be defined as a series of events repeated in the same order. Naturally, we start all over again, but the second time is different. The puzzle begins to grow to include more builders. No initiative can really be considered completed in one year. In order to scale the practice throughout the organization, the cycle must be repeated with a new constituency, new feedback, new revisions resulting in a new and better product. This work is as challenging as the first time in the cycle. It usually involves naysayers and reluctant participants which makes the work more difficult. Think of these players as the user interfacing with the prototype. From that analysis, both it and the designers iterate the design for a better, more accessible product. In many instances, the second time through the cycle will make or break the initiative. The preparation of the Rinse and Repeat stage is critical for the DEV leader. This is where evolution begins. The first time around was the burgeoning of an idea, repeating the cycle signifies progress on the pathway and creeping closer to scale.

CHAPTER 5
PAINTING MINEOLA'S PICTURE

Montage – An assembly of images that relate to one another in some way to create a single work or part of a work of art. A montage is more formal than a collage, and is usually based on a theme.

I didn't have an auspicious beginning to my superintendency. I was hired in 2009 by a 3-2 split board amidst a series of lawsuits between the former superintendent, a board member and a disgruntled, former employee. There were failed budgets, cuts in programs, and a growing sentiment to close schools. In fact that was my first task - not exactly the best case scenario. Since then, I've had the great privilege of being Mineola's superintendent for the last 13 years. We realized over time that painting a picture is more often a montage, rather than a snapshot. Our montage over the last 12 years can be categorized in four parts:

1. Reconfiguration
2. Experimenting and embracing technology to increase student engagement
3. Building our instructional model
4. Scaling the model

RECONFIGURATION

Mineola is an oddly shaped district (see Appendix 4). The geographic shape led to the construction of three small neighborhood schools (as part of the New Deal's Public Works Administration in 1939) to accommodate pockets of populations. A fourth elementary building was added in 1953. The concept of neighborhood schools made sense when there were enough children surrounding each building. As the population decreased, and the attendance zones changed, the concept of neighbors going to school with one another really didn't work. Over time, three of the four elementary buildings had 200 or less students, causing an "inefficient configuration that featured a replication and redundancy of services." That phrase was taken from a February 2008 report written by an outside consultant the Board hired to explore the possibility of closing schools. After a year of work, fact finding and public presentations, that Board and Superintendent decided not to move forward with the consultant's recommendation that Mineola should close at least one building.

This wasn't the first time the community had faced this dilemma; they closed a school three decades before (Appendix 4). It was a "Sophie's choice" decision that led to a lot of unhappy residents. Sometimes young parents have an inexplicable emotional attachment to their child's first school. Couple that with the unique culture that can form in each building and no one wants their school to close. So, when finances got better and new board members were elected, the school was reopened, even though there was no change in student enrollment. The situation was further complicated when they decided to build a brand new early childhood center in 2003. While the half-day kindergarten program went to full day, the numbers of students did not change. My leadership reality in 2009 was three buildings with less than 200 students in each, drastic inequalities in class size, and a budget that was driven by excess staffing. Intuitively everyone knew what needed to happen, but poor decisions in the past and a lot of sentimentality clouded people's vision. The first picture I had to paint was why it was important to reorganize the district.

During a Board of Education retreat one summer, the sentiment of the majority of the Board was that we needed to close schools. They also knew we needed a blueprint. We created a four part plan that would end up taking three years to actualize; our pieces to the puzzle.

PIECE 1: EDUCATING THE PUBLIC ON THE FINANCIAL FUTURE OF THE DISTRICT

It was decided that instead of telling the community that we need to close school we should educate them about district finances and possible scenarios if the statewide tax levy cap became a reality. At the time the discussion was about a 4% cap, but a 2% cap was enacted. The Board and I designed the community outreach plan for the financial future of Mineola. The outreach consisted of three town hall meetings with the following focus:

1. School Budgeting 101
2. The 2010-2011 Budget: What Should We Expect
3. Looking Forward: Budget Projections for the Next Three Years.

I launched a blog during this process entitled *Nagler's Notions*. This provided a social media outlet for people who could not attend. In addition, it became the forum for community discussion. The blog proved an innovative tool for community engagement and provided the Board with real time, vital information which they used in their decision making. Ultimately, the Board voted 4-1 to close two schools.

PIECE 2: DETERMINING AN EQUITABLE AND COST EFFICIENT DISTRICT CONFIGURATION

The new configuration had to affect every building in the district. Every resident had to have a stake in this plan, making it very different from the previous decision to close one building. The Board and I created the Community Committee on Consolidation or the Triple C. Parent and community involvement was a particular strength in the implementation of our reconfiguration. The creation of the Community Committee on Consolidation not only played a large role in creating the options for the reconfiguration, it also led to a grassroots organization being formed that promoted and explained the budget. The members of the committee included members from all of the stakeholder groups in the community. The only non-negotiable for the committee was to not repeat the mistakes of the past. The whole district needed to be reconfigured to avoid any animosity of one building bearing the brunt of closing.

The Triple C met every week for eight weeks and they became the experts on the issues surrounding the reconfiguration and worked hard to reach a compromise solution. After a consensus was reached, the committee made a presentation to the Board and the community (see Appendix 5). The committee sought to create a plan that honored the two divergent mindsets: keep neighborhood schools or cluster the entire district by grade bands (often called the Princeton Plan). The Triple C eventually reached a compromise configuration that created two pre-K through second grade buildings in the north and south of the district, neighborhood schools, then clustered grades three through five. How this would be accomplished and which buildings would remain open or closed was the next obstacle. The pieces started to fit together, and the discussion started to shift to *how* we should close schools rather than *should* we close schools.

PIECE 3: HOW WILL A SPLIT BOARD DECIDE WHICH OPTION TO CHOOSE

How does the Board make the right choice? Legally, the Board cannot abdicate its right to make a decision. So, they couldn't hypothetically send a survey to the community with three choices and then enact the option that received the most votes. The ultimate decision on how to reconfigure rested with them. How they ultimately determined which option to choose was quite innovative. The board decided to get input from the public via bond referendums. Since the elementary buildings were too small to accommodate more students, some capital work was needed to create any variation of the Triple C's compromise. The three main ideas that emerged were:

A. Close three schools and adopt a full Princeton Plan model. This would require building additions on two buildings and passage of a large bond to complete the work. The expenditure of 6.7 million dollars could yield savings three times that amount.

B. Close two buildings and create two K-2 buildings on opposite sides of the district and then adopt a cluster model of grades 3-5, middle school of 6-8 and the high school would remain the same. This plan also required a building addition and passage of a smaller bond to actualize the plan. The expenditure of 4.4 million would yield substantial savings as well.

C. Close two buildings, move the eighth grade to the high school (the building with the most room), create a 5-7 middle school, a 3-4 building and two K-2 buildings. This plan required no capital work and was labeled the Default Plan.

The final outcome really didn't matter to me. What was important was involving the whole community in the process.

The plan was simple: package all three options together and ask the public which one they wanted. We planned the most expensive option first with an October vote, the second most expensive for February and since the last choice didn't need a bond, it was the default option. The results of the referendums would inform the Board's decision on which option to ultimately choose and it provided a mechanism for community input. If the first bond failed, the board would put up the second. If that bond failed, the board would enact the default option. Ultimately, both bonds failed and the default option, which was the Triple C's recommendation, became the plan for reconfiguration.

ACKNOWLEDGE OBSTACLES AND JUMP HURDLES

As the bond votes were organized and presented to the public, it became clear from parent feedback in the southern portion of the district that their neighborhood school - Hampton Street - needed to remain open. We originally intended to keep the newest and most modern building (Willis Ave) in the south open. However, as we invited people to talk, we learned no one had an attachment to that building. We pivoted. We decided that Willis Avenue would be closed and Hampton would remain open. Unfortunately, Hampton wasn't big enough and needed an extension to be a viable choice. So, we gambled. We added $1.7 million to the May budget vote (instead of a separate bond) to actualize this new plan. This was a risky proposition since people had to reconcile spending more money when the purpose of closing schools was to save money. In addition, the southern portion of the district really didn't have a good history of voter participation. However, with record voter turnout, the budget passed.

Piece 4: Planning and Communicating How the Reconfiguration Would Be Accomplished.

When the budget passed in May there was not a lot of time to coordinate the closing of a school in September. This piece was the biggest challenge. It was imperative to communicate with parents and staff exactly how all of this would get done. Since the following year the district would close another building, the full implementation of the reconfiguration would take two years. Year one would concentrate on creating an 8-12 high school, a 5-7 middle school and making sure students would only make one transition to a new building. Year two would finalize the reconfiguration by creating a 3-4 building as well as two pre-K-2 buildings.

The first five years of my superintendency were spent actualizing this plan and dealing with the myriad of problems that arose. These problems included student transition plans, new bussing, new principals and staff, new cultures, excessing staff, renting the two closed buildings, new curriculum and professional development, and handling all of the bumps in the road from parents who didn't like the change. Even so, in the middle of all that chaos, I managed to begin an iPad initiative.

Experimenting and Embracing Technology to Increase Student Engagement

I had an epiphany early on in my superintendency - I had the authority to change things. Instead of lamenting about how things should be different, I realized I could actually be the change agent. If we were successful, we could be the exemplar others could emulate. Change in our little corner of the world could be impactful elsewhere. I analogize it to the first explorers - daring to go to places others were hesitant to explore. The excitement of the iPad and the burgeoning of instructional technology was the period in which my entrepreneurial side grew. I actively sought new and better ways to meet the needs of my kids. The iPad started the second painting in the montage.

The introduction of the iPad set off a series of DEV cycles that continually challenged our staff to iterate and experiment to change the way we thought about teaching and learning. In some cases, even after 10 years, we were still in a Rinse and Repeat step.

The iPad also opened up the vast resources of Apple, and the Distinguished School designation opened the doors for entrepreneurs to come to us. An entire network started to form in my state and Mineola was at the core. We hosted events for other schools and educators, we visited Cupertino, brainstormed with Apple executives, and helped start-ups launch products.

The Apple Distinguished School opened Mineola to the world of entrepreneurs and a global network that thrived on iteration and experimentation. I received many emails and phone calls from start-ups. One of our earliest partnerships was with eSpark. David Vinca (CEO) and I loved to brainstorm how the app could better serve learners. We had many meetings to discuss product development and next steps. David introduced me to Digital Promises' League of Innovative schools (DPLIS) and encouraged me to apply. Mineola's acceptance into the League opened a whole new national network of like-minded leaders. The more the network grew, the bigger and bolder the picture I was painting became.

We categorized and defined technology into four separate and discrete categories: assessment, instruction, management and communication. These categories helped us organize our initiatives and meet the varying needs of our school community. We launched NWEA as a counter balance to the new (and unproven) state exams and started a new standards-based student management system, School4One.

We failed, too. We had start-ups promise functionality in their apps they couldn't deliver. I rushed to implement a data cube that would allow us to triangulate the multiple data points that technology was now generating. The company we purchased from folded the year after we spent a lot of money and time creating the database. I got the district's money back on that one.

Of course there were many initiatives that weren't technology focused but were developed using the DEV cycle as well. Our dual-language program was started as an alternative to an ineffective Foreign Language in the Elementary School (FLES) program. We were early adopters for the Next Generation Science Standards and created a STEM class rotation that joined music, art and physical education as a "special."

All of these examples embraced the notion of experimentation. Build the idea, implement it, and see how it goes. Simultaneously, we developed champions for each initiative. It was the champions' responsibility to make sure the DEV cycle was followed and seek help if they couldn't jump the hurdles. The DEV cycle also dictates what initiatives will survive over time. The technology and apps may change, but with regular input from teachers and staff, adjustments are made and the programs typically grow and flourish.

Building Our Instructional Model

How often do you hear teachers complain about initiative fatigue? This is the notion that leaders are tone deaf to what is occurring in buildings and keep adding useless things to teachers' plates. It can also refer to a leader's inability to scale initiatives over time. Constantly chasing the next best thing will lead to initiative fatigue. Successful implementation of the DEV cycle allows leaders to determine the success or failure of an initiative. Moreover, it allows for adjustment which, in turn, allows for growth and scale.

My participation in DPLIS allowed me to visit many innovative school districts. Each visit generated new ideas and things I wanted to try in Mineola. FabLabs, TedEd, and pre-K badges are a few of the ideas from other League districts that we implemented and expanded through our DEV cycles.

We also uncovered some local partnerships that flourished into bigger initiatives. KidOYO, Queensborough College and Roble Media are three examples. All of these projects were launched simultaneously, some specific to a grade or school, some district-wide. During this period, we excelled at iteration and experimentation. All five buildings received the Apple Distinguished School award (they don't have a designation for the district). We were also identified as one of the top 25 most innovative districts in the United States by Successful Practices Network (SPN)/The School Superintendents Association (AASA). Nonetheless, we were nearing a saturation point that bordered on initiative fatigue. Right around this time I met Shawn Smith, CEO of Modern Teacher and our partnership with them helped us settle on our instructional model. Our model focuses on five main areas that are all intertwined while simultaneously independent. Use the QR code to the right to view a video on our instructional model.

Everything we launch and/or modify in a DEV cycle has to fit into one of these categories: integrated curriculum, computer science, assessment portfolios, flexible learning spaces, or growth mindset. Part 2 of this book dives into each of these areas.

The last part of our instructional model focuses on sharing. One of the big lessons we learned on our journey is that it is imperative to share what is happening in the classrooms. We challenged our teachers to show our community what our learners are doing. To accomplish this we created #MineolaProud. We encouraged, challenged and supported all staff to tweet pictures of what was happening in the classrooms. This, in turn, helped explain the value and importance of the instructional model. More importantly, it provided a mechanism for the school community to add a picture to the montage.

Scaling the Model

Our current picture involves the evolution of each part of the instructional model. What started out as a growth mindset has evolved into social emotional learning, brain science and zones of regulation. The badge book has evolved and grown with our original pre-K badge book learners. Our K-12 computer science program has added asynchronous coursework for which students can earn college credits. In addition, EVERY ninth grader challenges AP Computer Science Principles.

The pandemic didn't stop the work. DEV cycles continued, ideas continued to flow and we continued to plan. We are capitalizing on what worked for learners during the pandemic. We have changed and expanded our alternative high school to leverage asynchronous learning and allow students to pursue passion projects with the help of virtual mentors. DEV leaders find the silver lining in everything.

Although I would love to say I had this whole vision in my head when I took the job, I can't. What I can take credit for is thinking differently and creating a system that encourages responsible risk taking and celebration of mistakes. The reconfiguration of the district allowed for equity, everyone in the same grade experienced the same thing, it didn't matter which school you attended. The savings were also substantial, which allowed for a whole new series of innovations. It also stabilized our tax levy. Over the last 10 years we have averaged 1.42%. We have also accomplished over $65,000,000 in capital improvements without any bonds. Our first picture allowed the construction of a montage that has radically altered the learning experiences for students.

PART TWO

Introduction
Don't Take My Word For It

An idea without action will always stay just an idea. The same holds true for educational theory that is not put into practice - it's an untested concept. I'm a very practical person. If I'm not reading for pleasure, I read to learn and grow. My litmus test for educational books, journals and articles is simple: can I apply what I just learned? Is there meat on the bone? I understand the importance of theory and find it very useful, but I really want to see tangible, concrete examples of theory applied to real settings.

The second part of this book seeks to provide you with theory turned into practice. To accomplish this, I have asked a variety of people in our school community to provide examples of the work they participated in and/or created. All of these stories speak to EnR thinking and various stages of the DEV cycle. I hope these practitioner voices will lend credence to the theories described in the first part of the book. Each of the next five chapters is dedicated to each one of the tenets of our instructional model.   Integrated Curriculum, Assessment, Flexible Learning Spaces, Computer Science and Growth Mindset.

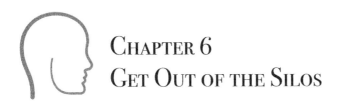

CHAPTER 6
GET OUT OF THE SILOS

"We busted out of class, had to get away from those fools. We learned more from a three minute record than we ever did in school."   *-Bruce Springsteen*

"When I think back at all the crap I learned in high school, it's a wonder I can think at all."   *-Paul Simon*

I believe that the institution of school slowly destroys the inquisitive nature of children and it seems to be happening faster. For years studies have shown a decrease of engagement in school as learners get older, usually when schools begin to departmentalize and over emphasize content memorization. (Brenneman, 2021) We tell kids what to learn regardless of their interest in learning it. Our systems cling to an archaic definition of being educated, namely there is a body of content across all disciplines that is necessary to learn. Those that learn it well are prepared for college, everyone else is doomed to a lesser existence, according to data correlating college degrees and salary. The current structure of high school, which is based on subject specialization, is dying a slow death. The ease of asking Siri and Alexa has raised the question of what should be taught in high school. I believe high school, as it is currently organized and conceptualized, will not exist in ten years. The change begins with integrating the subjects and asking students to apply the knowledge they have learned.

In New York State, this is easier said than done. Graduation requirements for students are based on Regents Exams - cumulative end of year content exams in four different subjects. Minimally, students must pass exams in one math (usually Algebra), one science, English language arts, global history and United States history. Advanced Regents Diplomas add two additional math (Geometry and Algebra II), an additional science as well as a world language. Integrating subjects that terminate in a Regents Exam is quite difficult, furthermore, it could be detrimental to a student.

How did we use EnR thinking to tackle this issue? It started with personnel, specifically getting more bang for the buck from our administrators. During the 2015-2016 school year, we decided to make a radical change in the administrative configuration of the district. After many conversations with Patricia Burns, my former Assistant Superintendent of Curriculum, we decided that in order to shift pedagogy we needed a new direction. We needed to shift emphasis from content specific subjects and start organizing around best instructional practice. Our professional development for teachers was building-based and disjointed. District-wide initiatives, like school reform movements, looked different in each building. Last, the PD opportunities for teachers always seemed to be content driven.

Below is an account written by Patricia on December 30, 2016, the day before she retired. The date is significant because her story predates my development of the DEV cycle - but her description captures all of the salient points and steps in the cycle.

EnR Thinking in Personnel: The Shift to Instructional Leaders
by Patricia Burns, Assistant Superintendent for Curriculum & Instruction
(retired)

Over the past few years, many school districts have spent time around developing curriculum that aligns with new Common Core standards. However, creating curriculum aligned with standards without looking at instructional practice is not enough to ensure improved student achievement. Research shows that "many schools lack an understanding of the changes needed [to achieve standards-based reform] and lack the capacity to make them." (National Research Council, 1999)

In Mineola, district and school administrators began a conversation about how to best support and sustain the most effective classroom instruction. We wanted to create a culture where every K-12 educator had the same high expectations for all students in all classrooms. We wanted to ensure that every student was engaged in learning from pre-kindergarten through high school. We realized that in order to accomplish this goal, we needed to break down individual, as well as department silos and work together to effect districtwide change. We also recognized that hit-and-run professional development was never the way to make long-lasting enduring changes. Research and common sense confirms that purposefully organized professional activities are the best way to support on-going learning.

We began to think about creating a new system in which the instructional leaders worked as a team to build the capacity to strengthen instruction in the entire school district. We decided to move away from the old paradigm of department chairs and elementary or high school specialists and shift to a new way of thinking. However, as Kirtman and Fullan (2015) explain in their book *Leadership: Key Competencies for Whole-System Change*, "the idea is not to be a rebel for the sake of it but to change the game from compliance to purposeful focus." At a point, the district and school-wide administrative team was revamped. Every school still had a principal, and the larger schools had assistant principals, however, the district now had a newly hired K-12 team of instructional leaders (IL). The role and responsibility of this newly formed team was to provide professional development throughout the year that focused on coherent instruction to engage students and make learning fun. The team would help build a shared culture of learning and set high expectations for all students to achieve. The team would also enable the district to comply with the new state Annual Professional Performance Review (APPR) regulations, as these instructional leaders would also conduct formal and informal teacher observations.

According to Fullan and Quinn "The senior leadership team must develop a common language and approach that is sustained and communicated consistently across the system." (Kirtman & Fullan, 2015) We began with an administrative retreat the previous summer which familiarized the new ILs with the mission of the Mineola School District. We introduced the infrastructure and systems established in the district. Then, we got to work. In year one, we decided to focus on three components in the Danielson Rubric: 1c, 1e and 1f. (Danielson & Axtell, 2009) We needed to build a foundation of understanding for every teacher in every classroom with a focus on coherent instruction, student engagement and designing formative assessments.

This new structure was to build on the establishment of school-based teacher leaders which we began the prior year. In 2015-2016, the district formed a collaboration with Teaching Matters to develop the capacity of classroom teachers to lead structured and outcome-focused grade level professional learning communities in their schools.

In the beginning, the structure seemed simple. The district established a cycle of meetings to ensure planning and communication. At the first meeting, the central office administration would meet with the principals and determine the specific needs for each school. At the next meeting, these needs would be communicated to the IL team and they would plan and prepare the professional development activities based on the needs of each school focused around the three pre-determined components in the Danielson Rubric. Finally, the principals and instructional leaders would meet with the teacher leaders to ensure a culture of continuous inquiry and learning.

Then, reality set in and we found that this "simple" structure was fraught with misconceptions and missteps. Some of the principals distanced themselves from the professional development, thinking that all professional learning was now determined by the central office administration and was the sole responsibility of the new IL team. Other administrators were biding time until the PD activities came to an end so they could have time with their staff for what "really mattered." The new IL team, unaware of the culture of each school, created uniform agendas only to discover that each school was in a different place in the learning curve. The teacher leaders felt that the new team was a new administrative team trying to take over the newly recognized responsibilities of the teacher leaders.

We soon discovered that with this new construct, there were problems, but they were fixable. We began with a series of one on one conversations with members of each constituent group to uncover the underlying issues so they could be voiced and addressed. The instructional leader team began to recognize the need to customize the PD plans and gain the respect and trust necessary to be effective in the schools. The school leadership slowly began to acknowledge that for instructional improvement to take hold, it had to be a whole team effort. This began with a shared sense of responsibility, open communication and collaboration, and trust which would, in time, result in clear and apparent outcomes.

$$\langle\!\langle\diamondsuit$$

As we concluded our fifth year with instructional leaders, I believe it was the single most effective move I have made so far in my thirteen years as a superintendent. This shift was a concrete example of EnR thinking deployed in an often overlooked area: personnel. By shifting the emphasis from subjects to instructional methodology, we witnessed an emergence of an entirely new culture. Changing the roles and responsibilities of traditional department chairs led to a new view of professional development, new teacher orientation, coaching and action research.

The Flexible Job Description

The instructional leaders' roles and responsibilities changed to meet the shift in teacher personnel. Each IL was responsible for a cadre of teachers (pre-K-12) that they formally observed. They also mentored a group of untenured teachers to ensure they were meeting district expectations for planning and implementation of district initiatives. Over time, we formed the new teachers into cohorts and developed a series of after school workshops based on action research in the classrooms. This four year sequence provided additional time to evaluate the progress of each teacher while simultaneously allowing them to earn in-service credits.

The ILs leveraged their individual expertise to research, design, and implement these new teacher workshops, but they also were responsible for designing and delivering professional development in the district (teachers are required to attend 18, 50-minute after school workshops throughout the year). When the people responsible for observing teachers actually design and deliver the PD, it is a very straightforward system. One key concept of our early work in instructional design is student choice. In fact, many new teachers studied choice as part of their action research projects.

Finally, each IL was assigned a project area that coincided with a district initiative including: elementary badge books, enrichment for all, design thinking/coding, RTI and reading literacy, new math curriculum, growth mindset, integrated curriculum and our partnership with Modern Teacher. As you can see, with one exception, they were NOT content driven.

The ILs have a home base at the central office and have locations at each school affectionately called bullpens. This avoids the perception that they have an allegiance to any particular building. The structure also ensures multiple contacts with our new teachers. This has proven invaluable when assessing the growth of staff; it becomes less about relationships and the personality of a teacher, and more about evidence of highly effective teaching.

The symbolic and functional result of reimagining department chairs has catapulted our ability to create new curricular units that integrate the disciplines pre-K-6.

The DEV Cycle for Integrated Curriculum: Advanced Literacies
by Catherine Shanahan, Instructional Leader

We started our integrated curriculum with a professional development course entitled Advanced Literacies. Advanced literacy refers to an expectation that all learners do more with text. As we know, in order to successfully participate in an ambiguous, 22nd century society, students are expected to read more complex texts to solve problems, create action plans, critique claims, and write and speak for diverse audiences. When I reflect on the development of the integrated curriculum, the hallmarks of advanced literacies stand out as its guiding force. In fact, they were the paint that was used to create our picture and vision. The success of the PD module, and the popularity among teachers, gained momentum in our Rinse and Repeat debrief at the end of the year. That momentum gave rise to a new minimum viable product, the framework of our grade level essential questions and integrated curriculum.

The development, implementation, and roll out of integrated curriculum in kindergarten through seventh grade is a clear example of the DEV cycle in action. In our initial design of the integrated curriculum, we drew a lot of our understanding of advanced literacies from researchers Lesaux, Galloway & Marietta. Their work explores how educators can develop these important skills with all learners, especially diverse, multilingual learners. These hallmarks became our why and what grounded us when we were met with obstacles, feedback and challenges throughout this entire process.

After determining our why and establishing a clear vision for the integrated curriculum, we began to create what-if scenarios by developing application of knowledge assessments, choice enrichment projects, coding activities and Socratic seminars. These were integrated into all of our units across K-7. Creating these learning opportunities was the fundamental task of the development team. Our puzzle piece quickly multiplied as we added additional pieces of specific curriculum objectives that we decided had to be integrated into the plan.

Our team of curriculum writers asked if incorporating these different learning opportunities ensured that our integrated curriculum aligned to the tenets of advanced literacies from the start. This sparked a lot of talking and feedback. Could kindergarteners really participate in Socratic seminars? How could sixth graders apply their knowledge of ancient civilizations through the essential question, how do turning points lead to change? As we reflected upon these and similar questions, we encouraged the curriculum writers to experiment, revise and reflect upon our work to test whether these particular learning opportunities aligned to the hallmarks of advanced literacies and, ultimately, to our vision. The DEV cycle was in full swing!

As with any initiative in which we attempt to bridge what we do and what we have to do, we needed to be explicit in how we were going to support students to achieve the expectations of advanced literacies in every unit. It was one thing to create and embed specific learning opportunities (like the ones mentioned above) into our curriculum that aligned to these hallmarks - what we have to do. It was another thing to prepare students to participate in them, which required us to draw on what we do. As we acknowledged this obstacle, the curriculum writers brainstormed, shared ideas and drew upon familiar research-based resources to help them determine the ways in which we were going to proactively support students to navigate complex texts independently. I encouraged this autonomy. It was ultimately decided that we would incorporate a close reading protocol that not only streamlined the teaching of complex text analysis and discussion skills but also aligned to the reading and writing expectations of high school.

Furthermore, teachers decided to embed text sets in the lesson sequences to help build students' conceptual knowledge of the social studies and science content that was taught in the unit. This strategy helped all students, especially diverse learners, to jump the hurdle of accessing grade level, complex texts in that subject area. In unit one, students in third grade learned about the traits of characters in fiction texts as well as the inherited traits of plants and animals as they explored how one's story was shaped by one's culture and geography. Students had an opportunity to apply the close reading protocol as they navigated a text set (non-fiction/fiction texts, videos, podcasts, pictures, etc.) that portrayed how characters, plants and animals were all affected by their unique settings. The unit culminated with students discussing their own answers using evidence from the text set. It is clear that the challenge of advanced literacies allowed the curriculum writers to seek opportunities to develop, implement and share resources that not only aligned to our why and big picture, but helped us to jump the hurdles that naturally arose throughout this process.

Feedback from assessments, teachers, and students pushed us to continue to develop the integrated curriculum. Our Rinse and Repeat debriefs continued to design even more opportunities for students to write for different purposes and for different audiences throughout all of our units. Fifth grade teachers supported students' understanding of how interactions can complicate things by including opportunities for students to write informational articles, in which they compared the characteristics of the three complex societies of the Western Hemisphere: Aztec, Incan and Mayan. During this same unit, students also presented an oral report for CNN Student News that explained which aspect of the Mayan, Inca or Aztec civilization MOST contributed to their success. They also created a sales pitch depicting how a chosen modern technology advanced our own society by making it more complex.

Each of these examples highlighted Mineola teachers participating in DEV cycles through EnR thinking. This initiative was a clear example of incremental, systematic change guided by leaders who were proactive in creating a pathway that led to a clear district vision. This vision was centered around supporting students' development of literacy skills needed to navigate an ambiguous, modern world. Check out our integrated curriculum with the QR code to the right.

The foundational work we did in our elementary grades provided students with the skills and flexibility to more readily deal with high school departmentalization. We began a new DEV cycle for an alternative high school we called Synergy. The goal was to develop a new type of high school that leveraged our expertise in asynchronous learning that allowed students to develop community connections in fields they were passionate about. Synergy provided an integrated curricular experience aligned with the Collaborative for Academic, Social, and Emotional Learning (CASEL) competencies that fostered student agency and academic success by offering choice in content, method, and pacing. They took the Regents Exams, but those assessments did not drive the content. Take a look at our video about Synergy with this QR code.

WHAT IS A 21ST CENTURY CURRICULUM?

The first part of this century introduced new curriculum concepts of blended learning, personalization and differentiation. As with many things in education, the terms are often co-mingled, even though they have very different meanings. They have also been met with some skepticism. The words may be new, but the concepts have been around for a while.

To begin to discuss personalized learning, we need to have a common definition which, like implementing school reform, garners different responses from educators. What is personalized learning? The answer seems to fall into one of three categories:
1. Using adaptive software that adjusts work and assessments to each learner's skill level
2. Systematic uses of data to inform decision making (i.e.: creating groups)
3. Increased student choice in projects and how they present their work

All three of these examples are often aligned with one of two schools of thought. One is the B.F. Skinner model, which emphasizes efficient mastery of content by using technology to continue to alter content and questions until the learner demonstrates proficiency in a specific topic. The other is the John Dewey model, which emphasizes finding a student's passion and interest and tailoring a pathway for them to explore and experiment. If those names sound familiar, they should. Both theories have been around since the 1950s. There really isn't anything new here, the game changer is technology. Technology makes all of the definitions doable and easy. Personalized learning must leverage the power and sophistication of technology and best pedagogical practice to create something new. (Herold, 2019)

In their book, *Personalized Learning: A Guide for Engaging Students with Technology*, the authors state, "Personalized learning is a 21st century model of differentiated instruction that addresses Tomlinson's and Allan's (2000) vision of addressing each student's readiness, interest, and learning profile through differentiation of content, process, and product." (Grant & Basye, 2014) Differentiated instruction has been lauded since the turn of the century, but the practice has not been easily embraced by the majority of teachers. The ability to pinpoint specific student deficiencies, then tailor work and resources for that student has remained elusive. The use of technology to help this process has given birth to the concept of personalization. Technology also allows for the expansion of *how* we teach and learn, which has given rise to the concept of blended learning.

Horn and Stacker's 2015 book, *Blended: Using Disruptive Innovation to Improve Schools*, defines blended learning as having three components:
1.   Any formal education program in which a student learns at least part through online learning, with some element of student control over time, path, and/or place.
2.   The student learns in part in a supervised brick and mortar location away from home.
3.   The modalities along each student's learning pathway within a course or subject are connected to provide an integrated learning experience.

Some might argue that the pandemic has introduced (and accelerated) the concept of blended learning, I would not. All three components must be present to call the practice blended. In many schools and districts, all three components were NOT present, but the pandemic has opened the avenue for a discussion - the opportunity to paint a picture. I believe the blended learning model will become more and more prevalent as an alternative to the traditional high school model.

Personalized Learning: The Mineola Way

Mineola's philosophy can best be described using the idea of an old railroad two-person handcar. Each person must work in tandem with the other to successfully move the handcar along the tracks.

We begin with the tracks, after all we need a foundation on which to travel. The first track represents our integrated curriculum and Regents level coursework. We have embedded student choice in all of our curricula, whether it be book clubs in a high school English class or a choice of assignments and assessments in our elementary schools. That first track is what schools would define as curriculum, in the traditional sense of the word. The second track, and equally as important, is the library of complementary applications (apps) and programs that allow for individual student work in skills and content. Curriculum isn't an app, and it is imperative that curriculum and technology complement each other for the benefit of the learner. The symbolism of the railroad track is purposeful to demonstrate the necessity of both schools of thought. The tracks represent the bridging of the Skinner model and the Dewey model making them interdependent of each other. Many districts combine the two and lose sight of the individuality necessary in each track. The two parallel and equally important tracks represent the learning pathway that every student and teacher must navigate successfully.

The handcar is a representation of the relationship between the student and the teacher. To propel themselves along the tracks, it is imperative that the people on either side of the hand crank give equal effort. From a student perspective they must know the areas they need to improve as well as the intended goals. The teacher must provide actionable feedback and direction in order for the student to excel. When the student and teacher are in sync and develop a rhythm, the progress and growth is easily visible. It is essential that the creation of the two tracks be a collaboration among and between teachers and administrators. These tracks provide a cohesive pathway on which every student will travel, BUT inherent in the design is personalization for each student.

There are three guiding principles that we use in the creation of this work:
1. Students need to know what they don't know
2. Students should try to solve real world problems
3. Students should have choice - in assignments and assessment

Know What You Don't Know

We presume, usually based on a number grade, that students know the specific skills with which they need help. How is a student supposed to improve and grow if they don't know what they are trying to improve? Many personalized learning apps benchmark students using a pre-assessment, drill-and-kill the deficient area, then retest. If the score goes up, growth has been accomplished. In general, there is nothing wrong with this methodology as long as it compliments a robust and diverse curriculum. Additionally, the tasks students are asked to complete should be engaging and age appropriate. For example, an eighth grade student reading on a third grade level should not be given content designed for a third grader. The latest version of ELA apps provide the same article at varied reading levels. The most critical piece of this tenet is not the process of benchmarking, it is the quality of the feedback provided to the student. It also requires a new examination of grading policies as well, a clear understanding of the learning standards. Teachers must have specific look-fors when determining if and when a student is making progress in the standard. I provide more detail in chapter 7 when I discuss deliberate practice.

Check out this QR code for more information on the Learning Zone .

Real World Problems

Kids often disengage when they don't see a connection between what they learn in school and what they experience outside of school. This is particularly relevant for high school students nearing graduation. Life after high school can be scary and it is up to the school district to create and adjust programs to provide students with the opportunity to secure work that provides more than a minimum wage. Our ultimate goal is for every student to attend college, but we also know that goal isn't feasible. So, we compromise. We bring them to college in their senior year. Mineola High School Principal, Dr. Whittney Smith, describes the high school's model.

The DEV Cycle for College Partnership:
Computer Science and Internship Strand
by Whittney Smith Ed.D., Principal, Mineola High School

Real vs. relevant. Transforming learning at the high school level is often viewed as a difficult task. In New York State, high school graduation requirements include specific coursework and a number of summative assessments called Regents Exams. This combination of course credits and examinations determine whether a student graduates and is the driving force in the curriculum of the classes. The rote nature of these exams, albeit changing with the New Framework Exams, drives many teachers to cover the content, rather than teaching the skills and then empowering the students to research the content and demonstrate their learning. It is necessary that school leaders create opportunities for students to develop real skills for the world they will be entering. While I am proud that we have instituted 1:1 learning with iPads, and have twice been acknowledged as an Apple Distinguished School, I am even more proud of the teaching and learning that has transformed our school. Our students are empowered, our teachers embrace the 4 Cs, and the learning has shifted from consumption to creation. We still needed more for our students.

At Mineola High School, a suburban high school on Long Island, college and career readiness has taken on a whole new meaning. While we offer a host of options for our students including multiple elective classes, we wanted to offer a specific direction for students. A strand that leads to both a high school diploma and a college certificate, coupled with real world experience. The goal is to develop in our students these life skills: complex problem solving, critical thinking, creativity, people management, coordinating with others, emotional intelligence, judgment and decision making, service orientation, negotiation, and cognitive flexibility.

After looking at our community college persistence data and number of students requiring remedial coursework upon entering college, we knew we needed a better plan. One that could prepare them for their future in an ever-changing market. In a market where the jobs we prepare them for either do not exist, or are in fields with which our current system is not familiar. Jon Oringer, founder and CEO of Shutterstock, reminds us, "There is a lack of talent in technology, and we need to be encouraging kids in school to learn how to code. We need to encourage computer science as a major. We need to encourage entrepreneurism."

We also needed an increased focus on student interests. Where did we start? We wanted to identify a field of study that provided students with an excellent experience that would either ignite a passion for further study in college or prepare them to enter the workforce. We also wanted an area that would allow students, once interested, to choose from a wide range of opportunities in the chosen field of study. We began with computer science where students were interested, and the job outlook was bright.

We knew we needed partners in higher education as well as the business world in order to make this dream a reality for our students.

We planned to launch this program with "Cohort A" in the next school year and needed to prepare. We spent a great deal of the previous year working out the college articulation agreement and planning to serve the students in a cohort-type program. We needed to backwards plan, beginning with the end in mind while involving our stakeholders in the entire process in order to establish buy-in. What courses could we teach at the high school? What courses needed to be taught at the college? Did we have the right teacher or did we need to hire someone? How would the students get to and from the college? How would we identify students? We knew we had the support of our Board of Education, in fact three of their goals were:

1. Develop and implement a four-year plan to align high school coursework and partnerships in specific Career and Technical Education (CTE) strands.
2. Explore partnerships with local universities to offer certificate programs to our students during their senior year.
3. Continue to develop and encourage students to engage in college level coursework.

Our Superintendent attended all of the planning meetings and supported this program in every imaginable way. We would often have conversations in our offices, at the college, on the phone, and in the car traveling to and from the college campus. He was all-in. In fact, he even helped facilitate an internship program to round out the students' experience.

Recruitment of both the right teacher as well as the right students was essential. We conducted an exhaustive search, and hired a dynamic teacher with an extensive computer science background. We also had multiple outreaches within our district to explain the program and opportunity it would provide for our students and community.

The program was designed for students to complete as a cohort, during their junior and senior year. We embedded coursework into our Technology 8 class (our high school begins in the eighth grade). We also added AP Computer Science Principles for all students in the ninth grade as well as opportunities in robotics in order to keep an eye on interest and identify potential candidates early on in their high school career.

In a student's junior year, they completed dual enrollment courses in Operating Systems and Systems Deployment, Web Technology I, and Web Client Programming: JavaScript. Students also completed pre-calculus at the high school in addition to their science, English, social studies, and other high school requirements. We worked within the confines of a nine period day. Students took their high school requirements during periods 1 through 4 and their college courses (at the high school) periods 5 through 9.

In their senior year, students followed the same structure but were taken by bus to the college campus. During the afternoon time slot (10:30-2:20) they took Network Fundamentals I, Introduction to C++, Personal Computer Technology, Architecture, and Troubleshooting (A+ Certification) as well as Economics.

The final piece to truly solidify a college and career readiness experience was to create a meaningful internship experience for our students. We looked to our friends at Core Business Technology Solutions for their expertise. They were on board from the moment we mentioned it. We conducted multiple focus group meetings that once again included our Superintendent, Assistant Superintendent, Guidance Director, Principal, and Core Team to hash out our vision and logistics. Core was able to provide three experiences the students would rotate through over the course of the school year.

This year-long internship experience took place in periods 5 through 9 on the days that students do not have class on the college campus. In the tech services cycle, students worked with our district technicians, learning about network operations, hardware, software, and the tech ticket system with hands-on experience. In the marketing cycle, our students met virtually using Cisco TelePresence in our school with the marketing team at Core to develop strategies to use with the company's programs. Finally, on the sales/business side of the operation, students were taken to Core's office to work with the business team on site. All of the students were treated like real employees of the company and wore uniform shirts and ID badges.

We have grown to think that real is even more important than relevant. We have prepared our students for their future through this unique program and gave a whole new meaning to College and Career Readiness. See our video on College and Career Readiness through the QR code to the right.

This program has been so successful that we have begun to replicate it in several other areas: Entrepreneurship, Advanced Manufacturing, and Healthcare. The process is the same for all three. Begin with the end in mind, find a partner in higher education, find a business partner, then develop your cohort. Be patient, anything new takes time. Remember, EnR!

CHOICE - The Fifth C

I would argue that choice is the biggest and most frequently overlooked part of personalization. As technology grows exponentially, so does the ability to allow students a voice and choice in the content they consume and the method in which they demonstrate understanding.

Both of my children started their education in a Montessori school. They were part of a multi-age classroom filled with hands-on centers that challenged their curiosity. The hallmark of a Montessori program is an individual learning plan (ILP). Each week the teacher created the ILP and outlined the work she wanted each learner to complete. The order did not matter, nor did the time of the day they did the work, each child decided how and why they tackled the plan. My wife and I were allowed to visit the classroom behind two-way mirrors and watch our kids work and play with others. It was truly amazing to see: 4 and 5 year olds managing to be self directed, curious, decision makers and owning their own learning. Maria Montessori understood the power of choice.

Student agency, the ability for a learner to have voice and choice, has gained momentum in the 21st century. Technology has certainly played a role in its development. In fact, there is probably a YouTube video explaining it! Learning in the technology age takes on a whole new meaning. The availability of free digital content AND the ability for learners to create their own digital content has changed the teacher/student dynamic. So, why do we insist on telling children what and how to learn? There is a shift in the classroom power dynamic that will change the way we teach and learn. Please don't misunderstand this to mean we do not need teachers - we do - but their role must change. Like a Montessori program, teachers should create learning plans for students and help them set goals to actualize the plan. Teachers can guide students on what materials they would like to use as well as how they will demonstrate their understanding. The shift moves the ownership of learning to the learner.

The DEV leader's role in choice is to challenge teachers to understand the need for the power dynamic shift. Homework is probably the best example. The original intent of homework was to reinforce the daily lesson, but what if a learner mastered the daily lesson? Why do they need to do homework? If the learner can demonstrate they understand the work, shouldn't that be enough? Of course, technology helps with this dilemma. Programs like Khan Academy can track the amount of time a learner spends working on skills and can place them at an appropriate level. It is common for a weekly homework assignment to be to complete 30 minutes on Khan for the week. Not only can learners choose when to do this, they usually log more than the required time.

EnR Thinking:
Making Something Out of Nothing, Our Dual Language Program
by Nicole Moriarity, Ed.D.

Mineola has an established pre-K-10 Dual Language Program. To get here, we have been in a DEV cycle for eight years and we continue to engage in the Rinse and Repeat phase with each new year. I have been the leader of this journey from the beginning. A journey of failures, innovation, and going through the cycle.

Nearly two years before new English as New Language (ENL) regulations (CR Part 154) were adopted in New York State, we set out to begin the design thinking process by exploring the question: How might we provide bilingual education at Mineola and support learners in their home and target languages? The first configuration came with the development of a Spanish Immersion Transitional Bilingual Program. Throughout the year, the team met and discussed their experiences, observations, and data. From this they drew two conclusions. First, supporting learners in their first language was one of the most important and profound pedagogical shifts we could make to support our learners. Second, Spanish Immersion Transitional Bilingual Programs separated students from their peers, leaving them with a feeling of isolation. In our attempt to better educate and be inclusive, we were actually leaving our learners with a sense of not belonging to the larger school community. What makes this configuration so special is that we failed. Yes, we failed! This failure is what helped us move forward. The Rinse and Repeat cycle was officially in full effect.

Our question shifted to: How might we provide bilingual education at Mineola and support learners in their home and target languages while creating the conditions essential for academic and social success in school? Armed with our new question and with an enthusiasm for engaging in this creative problem solving, Mineola widened the committee to include other representatives. What happened next was a journey that twisted and turned, required many revisions, and never really ended. It was fascinating to metacognitively be aware of the DEV cycle as we were actively participating in it. In fact, the word fascinating is the adjective we used every time we reflected.

The first stage was to learn as much as we could. We were ravenous, tearing through books and workshops. Through this stage of acquiring knowledge we could begin to truly conceptualize what we were looking to create. We discovered an abundance of research indicating two-way bilingual education programs were, in fact, more effective at achieving language acquisition in both languages, maintaining academic rigor and supporting students socially. How would we accomplish this as we would need each class to be 50% English dominant and 50% Spanish dominant learners? How would we continue to support the learners as they progressed through the grades? After all, we did not want the program to end any earlier than sixth grade. Which led us to ask: How could we support our learners all the way through to graduation so they could earn a biliteracy seal on their diplomas? Finally, we asked if we really needed a weak FLES program with a very strong dual language program in place?

By giving us a common purpose, we generated more ideas and more questions causing us to want to experiment more and create more. The next school year, still one full year prior to the adoption of the new regulations, we embarked on an ambitious plan: beginning a K-2 dual language program in which students could enroll even if they did not begin in kindergarten. To begin our recruitment process, we coalesced around our why, then articulated it to all of our parents and learners. While other districts were trying to figure it out, Mineola was well on its way to hiring bilingual staff members at the elementary

81

and secondary levels. We believed we could anticipate the needs of our learners and Dual Language Program and could begin planning with each new retirement by hiring bilingual teachers, social workers, guidance counselors, and clerical staff members. Yet, we still continued to fail. This is where our true learning occurred. With every failure, we gained new insight and a new solution to a problem that we might not even know existed. We were failing forward and continuing with the rinse and repeat cycle.

After the recruitment process kicked off for bolstering enrollment, we faced many other hurdles. The list was exhaustive such as how to allocate language: a half-day model, day-to-day, 6-day cycle, or week-to-week. How did we ensure the teachers we were hiring were highly effective and would deliver the best educational experiences for our learners? Would they be empathetic and cognizant of the many factors that impacted the learner profiles of multilingual learners, immigrants and Students with Interrupted Formal Education (SIFE)? How could we make sure the parents of our learners were actively engaged in the educational process and supporting their children as well as the Dual Language Program? Once again, fueled by curiosity and a propensity to engage in design thinking, we were repeating our rinse cycle. We created a parent committee, with representatives from each grade level and each school. They brought us more questions and we solved problems together. Through continued research we fine-tuned our language allocation model and began to elevate the Spanish language in our schools. We developed newcomer programs and embedded social emotional learning into academic objectives.

As the school year progressed, with the addition of the Dual Language Program in the third grade, we met and analyzed our work. We continued to ask more questions. How could we ensure the language allocations are equally distributed among all of the content areas? How could we engage in biliteracy pedagogical practices to ensure the development of biliterate learners? How could we ensure that the Dual Language Program was not an afterthought? How would we ensure that students remain in the program through high school and beyond? These questions led us to seek out professionals in the field who could provide us with more professional development. We continued to read articles, books, blogs, and engage in twitter chats. Essentially, we continued the DEV cycle with each new interaction. Basically, engaging in the cycle supported us in solving multiple problems in a proactive and positive manner. Instead of asking what we could do or how we could do it, we asked how we might provide bilingual education at Mineola and support learners in their home and target languages. Thus, leading us down the path of creativity and innovation.

As of the writing of this vignette, we continue our inquiry and the DEV cycle continues as the entire dual language staff meets in a district-run biliteracy institute designed entirely by the staff members who volunteer for the Dual Language Steering Committee. Now, entirely driven by the staff and parents, the Dual Language Program will continue to evolve and grow into something that is greater than ever imagined!

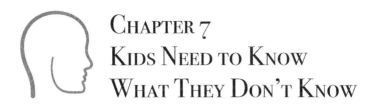

CHAPTER 7
KIDS NEED TO KNOW
WHAT THEY DON'T KNOW

"Not everything that counts can be counted, and not everything that can be counted counts."   *- Albert Einstein*

Picture a dog chasing its tail. Visualize him spinning around and around, becoming dizzy in the process. If he eventually bites his tail, he yelps in pain, but that doesn't stop him from doing it again. That's how I feel about grade level standardized tests. As leaders we are judged by how our students do on tests, so we chase results - even when we know we shouldn't do it. I am not against standardized exams, I believe they are necessary. I am against using one single indicator to determine a child's ability. It is not fair to kids, teachers, schools, or districts to rank and sort using one measure.

I like the example Tom Murray uses in his book *Personal and Authentic: Designing Learning Experiences That Impact a Lifetime* (Murray, 2019). He uses a football player's scouting report after the National Football League (NFL) combine. The scouting report highlighted the drawbacks to a certain player's negatives: poor build, very skinny and narrow, ended the 1999 season weighing 195 pounds and still looked like a rail at 211, looks a little frail and lacks great physical stature and strength, can get pushed down more easily than you like, lacks mobility and ability to avoid the rush, lacks a really strong arm, can't drive the ball down the field and does not throw a really tight spiral, system type player who can get exposed if he must ad lib. and do things on his own.

Murray ponders,

> What didn't the standardized testing at the NFL combine measure?
> The tests used for all players leading up to the draft couldn't measure

Tom Brady's work ethic. They didn't measure his fierce competitiveness or his leadership abilities. No test at the NFL combine measured Brady's ability to persevere, his resiliency, or his burning desire to win. It is these things, things that weren't measured and couldn't be measured by a standardized test, that made Brady one of the greatest NFL players of all time. (Murray, 2019)

Murray's observation is a perfect example of the pitfalls of using a single assessment to judge or predict future success. A logical solution seems to simply use multiple measures to capture a larger, more inclusive picture of a person's strengths and negatives, not focused on one or the other. Yet, our society rejects multiple measures for the more convenient ranking and sorting that is accomplished using standardized exams. The emphasis on rank has been detrimental to school reform and changing school systems. This obsession has a direct impact on teaching and learning in our country.

In her book *Learner Centered Innovation: Spark Curiosity, Ignite Passion and Unleash Genius* (Martin, 2018), Katie Martin describes it in this way,

In an era where test scores and test prep dominates conversations, educators feel compelled to stick to the curriculum and cover it all, and we work to convince ourselves that we have "prepared" students by teaching them how to take tests. Most educators know in their hearts, however, that there is far more to teaching than success on the test, which puts them at odds with what is measured and how they are held accountable.

Therein lies the problem. DEV leaders know we *must* look at assessment differently or we cannot move the needle on changing teaching and learning. Knowing and doing are very different things. This is why DEV leaders must actively find alternate means of assessment in which the desired outcome for students is to be creative, think critically, communicate effectively and collaborate. The mindset of assessment, specifically tests, in our country has not changed in decades. We cling to the traditional mindset of content directed tests. Whether state assessments or locally created formative assessments, the tests are based on content memorization and sophisticated understanding of language and nuance.

Consider the following: If I was able to tell you all about the battles in both arenas of the Civil War and explain the strategic significance of each, but I couldn't remember the generals' names, would I pass your test? To answer the question we would need to know the type of exam you administered. If you gave a traditional multiple choice, fill in, short response or even a document-based question (DBQ) my chances of passing may be diminished. If you allowed me to make a short video, create a website or even write a play, you would have a better understanding of my grasp of the content. Is that not the ultimate goal?

How do we shift how we think about assessment? The first step is to agree that multiple measures of student knowledge are better than any single indicator. **If we can commit to using a combination of measures, all with equal weight, we can radically change most of our debilitating institutional practices**.

Multiple measures automatically change the dynamic of teaching to a test. If multiple measures exist then the issue of assessment driving curriculum would be radically altered. The emphasis would shift from rote memorization of content to actually demonstrating your understanding of what was taught. James, my 14 year old son, recently took an online AP course. When I asked him how his teacher knew he was actually doing the work he replied, "The DBA." This piqued my curiosity, what is a DBA? I had never heard of that. Turns out, every week his instructor held a discussion-based assessment - DBA. Astonishing! The teacher simply asked James to explain the concept and content taught, either he knew it or he didn't. More importantly, he received instant, specific feedback on the next steps of his learning pathway. Why is such a simple concept so difficult to implement?

The answer lies in the commitment to an evolution in assessment, not a revolution. Any radical, abrupt change will be met with resistance and will, most likely, stymie efforts. Instead we need to take clear, concise steps toward a new multiple measure framework. I have outlined seven steps toward this journey, all of which do *not* eliminate the existing structures. Instead, the steps are designed to work simultaneously with existing practices to give ample time to evolve into a new assessment framework.

ADAPTIVE TESTING

Advances in technology have led to computerized exams that adapt to the user based on how the students answer the questions. If a student gets the answer wrong the next question is pulled from a data bank of questions of similar or lesser difficulty. The test continues, constantly changing questions, challenging the student based on their performance. Eventually, the test narrows the performance to a zone of proximal development and creates a benchmark in specific content and skills. The result is a starting point for each student accompanied by a target goal for the next exam. Adaptive tests require less time to administer and are designed to be given two or three times in a school year. Critics of adaptive testing suggest the exams are problematic because all students are not completing the same items or exposed to the same content in the same manner, they would favor norm referenced exams.

Norm referenced exams compare one student's score in relation to another student that is similar in age, grade, individualized education program (IEP), English language learner (ELL), etc. The results of norm referenced exams establish a bell curve, with a mean of 50%. Half of the students that take the exam will be below average. One of the major issues with standardized, norm referenced exams is the ranking aspect of the score reports. Also important to note is that since we don't have a national exam, comparisons among and between state exams are not easily transferable.

State exams may or may not be labeled as norm referenced, but essentially many are treated the same way. The New York State (NYS) content-based criterion Regents Exams are a perfect example. Students must pass five of these exams in four different subjects to graduate. When I took the exams in the 1980s each question had an assigned point total, the points added up to 100, and your grade was determined by adding up the points associated with the questions you answered correctly. Today, Regents Exams are not scored that way. Instead, scores are calculated using a scaled score method. The percentage of correct answers are placed on a predetermined scale to calculate a final score. It is possible to obtain a score of 65 and only get 45% of the answers correct.

In essence, the state can determine the overall passing rate on the exam before any students take the test. The NYS Regents Exams are a perfect example of trying to fit a square peg in a round hole and begs the question: what is the purpose of exams? If the desired goal is for students to master content specific curriculum why would you scale the results? That puts aside the value and purpose of memorizing content in the age of the internet. More importantly, what skill(s) are these exams measuring? Are they any indication of success after high school or are they merely a mechanism to determine graduation?

Adaptive exams, unlike norm referenced exams, provide a benchmark that is specific to each student. However, like norm referenced exams, they also establish a percentile rank for each student or how well a student performed in comparison to the students in the specific norm group, such as in the same grade and subject. These two pieces of information form the discussion about growth and proficiency.

Growth AND Proficiency

An article in the Christian Science Monitor (Hinckley, 2018) stated,

> The word "proficient" is often used to mean suitable, apt, or at best, competent. An amateur cook, student driver, or French 101 student, for example, might describe his or her skills as proficient. But the National Assessment of Educational Progress (NAEP) – the only national assessment in the United States since 1990, used as a barometer of student achievement – defines proficiency as "demonstrated competency over challenging subject matter," which experts interpret as high achievement. This mismatch in definitions causes a lot of confusion when it comes to analyzing scores from "The Nation's Report Card" every two years. On Tuesday, for example, when NAEP's 2017 scores were released, it was again evident that analysts and journalists use proficiency as the bar for success, citing that only 30 to 40 percent of 4th and 8th graders in the US are "proficient" in math and reading. Critics say NAEP's far-reaching definition of "proficient" can directly impact students' education through inflated standards in widely used curricula like Common Core, low morale among teachers and administrators, and

unnecessary confusion and disappointment for average Americans. Students in the US are actually improving, say observers, especially over the long term, and NAEP's nomenclature can shroud legitimate progress that has been made in education.

Not only is the term proficiency ambiguous, the concept is flawed. We establish imaginary proficiency or grade levels based on the average of similar students, then we work to raise everyone that falls below that line to eclipse the line. Not only is this mathematically impossible, it ignores the implied purpose, measuring student achievement. In order to measure achievement each student must have a starting point and then we must measure each student's growth over a specific time period.

In order to ascertain student proficiency we need to understand student growth. Using one measure in the absence of the other does a disservice to all of our students. If your doctor told you your blood pressure was 120, should you be worried? You wouldn't know because there is a vital piece of information missing. Blood pressure is composed of two numbers. The first number, systolic, measures the flow of blood when the heart is pumping. The second number, diastolic, measures the flow of blood when the heart is resting. Both pieces of information are critical to getting an accurate measurement and using only one number doesn't give you a full picture. Once both measurements are calculated you then can make a determination of whether or not your blood pressure falls within an acceptable range. The relationship between both numbers is critical in making a diagnosis and simple metrics are used to determine whether or not your pressure is normal, elevated, high or hypertensive. I argue that student achievement should be determined using the same methodology.

We don't recognize and report student growth, but it must be established as a tenet of student achievement. Whether a student falls above or below the proficiency line there must be a value-added metric to their educational experience. What a student learned over the course of the school year *and* how growth was demonstrated should be the focus of student assessment. The efforts that students and teachers make to move from point A to point B is a more valuable metric than whether or not a student reaches a proficiency level.

However, it is equally important to establish the bar you are working toward, hence the need for both numbers.

For example, John took an adaptive exam in September that established a benchmark score for him as well as a target goal for the next exam to be given in January. John's teacher examines the results of the exam as well as John's actual work in his goal areas. If John's benchmark score and his actual work are in congruence, the teacher determines the work (learning plan) necessary for John to meet his target goal. John's teacher also notes that his target goal, if met, would still not place him as proficient, but John's learning plan to meet his target growth is rigorous and appropriate. When the January adaptive test is administered John and his teacher review his results. The score report, coupled with John's work and effort in class, should reflect John's growth toward meeting his target goal as a function of reaching a proficiency level. Hypothetically, if John met his goal (100%), but still falls short of a proficiency benchmark (75%), he would receive 100/75 as his score. Conversely, a high achieving student that is complacent, tends to put forth minimal effort, and doesn't meet their target goal may receive a 75/100.

By making growth and proficiency interdependent you eliminate the need to rank students and schools based on the performance of similar groups. Instead, you can establish acceptable ranges of performance, similar to the blood pressure scale.

	Growth		Proficiency
Normal range	Over 65%	and/ or	Over 65%
Elevated	Between 25-60%	or	Less than 65%
High	Between 0-25%	or	Less than 50%

Numbers are for illustration purposes only.

The blood pressure analogy is designed to make the argument of the importance of marrying student growth and proficiency. I am sure a psychometrician would find flaws in my examples and percentages. The intention is to rethink how we measure student achievement and identify schools that fall short in both growth and proficiency.

To this point we haven't examined the best assessment tool we have: student work

BADGES

Actualizing a standards based report card in pre-K and kindergarten proved to be a daunting task. We found it very difficult to place children on the continuum of progress in meeting the standards. In addition, parents found the report card cumbersome and confusing. I was introduced to the concept of badges after visiting the Elizabeth Forward School District outside of Pittsburgh, PA. After a few runs through the DEV cycle, we created a badge book for pre-K, similar to a common sticker book, to replace our report cards.

We reimagined our report card system to focus on our students' growth and development over the course of their kindergarten year. Instead of grades, kindergarteners earned badges, in the form of stickers, to recognize mastery of new skills and concepts. Students earned badges at their own pace, based on their individual strengths, needs, and developmental levels. The goal was for students to own their own success and speak to the skills they mastered. The book provided detailed descriptions of each badge skill, criteria students needed to meet to earn the badge, and resources and activities that helped students practice. Parents used the information in the badge book to be a part of their child's learning. The badges and the book gave students a clear way to understand and take ownership of their learning. See what the Badge Books look like through the QR code to the right.

The overall reaction to the badge book from parents, teachers and students was such a resounding success we expanded the concept to first and second grade. As children advanced, the standards became more complex and multi-faceted. We needed a way to separate the standards into discrete parts to help students and parents see the specific skills associated with each part of the standard, but not lose sight of how the pieces were connected. We invented new learning pathways for several anchor standards. A pathway is a collection of micro-badges that, when they are all earned, comprise a mastery badge. We asked our grade level teachers to tackle this problem. Below is Teacher Leader, Samantha Sanchez's story.

My Role in the DEV Cycle of the Second Grade Badge Book
by Samantha Sanchez, Teacher Leader

Before Badge Books, we graded our learners using report cards three times a year. The report card grades would be posted on our Parent Portal, the parents would view them, and the kids would come back to school the next day without any understanding of the report card grades. The grades were 1-5, so even if a learner knew what they had received for a standard, what did that mean to them? Probably nothing. Report cards and conversations surrounding report cards left out the most important people: the learners!

How do you involve the most important people? You create a standards-based badge book that makes sense to kids. I absolutely loved the idea of a badge book from the moment I heard about it.

The Badge Book was a system that would make sense to teachers because we created it using the Next Generation Science Standards (NGSS) standards and connected it to our integrated curriculum. It made sense to parents because it was written in a way that everyone could understand what the standard was asking of the learner. Most importantly, it made sense to kids because they were at the forefront of each conversation surrounding its creation! Suddenly, our learners were part of the equation. Children would know what they needed to know so they could grow. The conversation of grades (who got a 3, who got a 5, what is a 5) would shift and all of our conversations with learners and families would focus on growth.

As a Teacher Leader in Mineola, I had the privilege of being part of the first and second grade Badge Book committees. Our learners already had experience with the Badge Book in pre-K and kindergarten and by the time they were in first grade, they were pros! This also meant we (the teachers) were lucky enough to have two grade levels to help us develop the first grade book, and three grade levels to help develop the second grade book!

Each time the Badge Book moved up a grade level, we shared experiences, successes, failures and new ideas on how to revise the book to make sense to learners in our grade levels. We dove into the standards. We had lengthy conversations about what they meant and how to get our learners to understand what they needed to do. We figured out how to change the structure of our classrooms so students were able to work on the badges they still needed to earn.

As we continued to move forward with the Badge Book creation process for second grade, we quickly realized that the standards became more complex. Because the standards required more from our students we introduced the idea of a pathway in our second grade Badge Book.

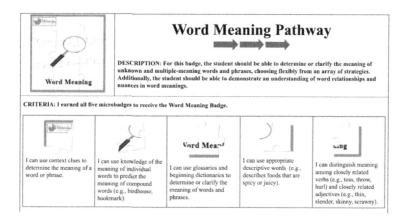

In a pathway, there are multiple skills that must be learned to reach the Mastery Badge. Micro badges for each skill can be earned in any order and mastery can be demonstrated at any time, but *all* micro badges in the pathway must be earned. Breaking up certain standards into micro badges allows learners, teachers, and families to know exactly what skill the learner is working on and what skills have already been mastered.

Creating the Badge Book as a committee was a lot of fun and a great learning experience for each person involved. Implementing the Badge Book was going to be really tough. At least, that's what I thought before I actually did it. The thought of assessing over 60 badges for all of my learners that were all at different places seemed close to impossible.

However, if we really believed (and we did) that each learner should earn badges at their own rate based on their unique strengths, needs, and developmental levels, we had to work together to find a way to make it happen.

Our grade level Professional Learning Communities (PLCs) met weekly and we continuously discussed how to involve learners in the process, how to make connections between badges and integrated curriculum, ways to modify and improve assessments, what constituted a badge, how to enrich learners once they earned a badge, how to create centers based on the badges, and much more. Our conversations always focused on the growth of our students and creative ways we could support our learners as they worked towards their badges.

We were able to try, fail, try again, succeed, reflect and try something new over and over again - just like the learners do when working towards a badge.

The beauty of the Badge Book is that learners always know what badges they are working on. They frequently look at their Badge Book to reflect on what they earned and what they still need to work towards. The learners make a plan to earn the badge and practice independently because they know what they have to do. They are responsible for their learning, have autonomy and are invested in their learning and progress.

The badges made me a better teacher for my students. Because students progress after mastery of a badge, I always knew what skill each of my learners were working on. Therefore, I was able to create opportunities for them to continue practicing those skills.

The Badge Books also made my students more independent. My students spoke about the badges and felt a sense of accomplishment whether or not they earned the badge. The learners viewed everything as growth. It was a wonderful thing to see a student work really hard to learn a skill, tell you that they are ready to earn the badge, then earn it! The learner put their sticker or stamp right in the book. That tangible representation of learning a skill made sense to them and they were proud of their hard work. If they did not earn the badge, they put a neuron stamp in place of the badge sticker and continued working towards that skill.

In a Badge Book classroom you will see this process:

- Celebrate badges earned (badge sticker/stamp)
- Identify what you don't know and celebrate progress (neuron stamp)
- Create a plan to earn a badge (how to practice, identify resources)
    ◦ Example: I want to earn my Fluency Badge. To earn this badge I have to be able to fluently add and subtract within 20. I can create index cards with fluency facts, practice my partners to 10, and use a math app like Reflex Math
- Assess or reassess the skill (earn the badge or neuron stamp)
- Reflect and make a new plan

Even though our district has been implementing Badge Books for four years, our work is not even close to being done.

We continue to find ways to involve the learners in every part of the Badge Book process. We continue to ensure that we are speaking with our learners about their growth.

We learn from each other and implement the Badge Books in new and more innovative ways every year. Teachers have created centers, checklists, reflection pages, goal setting pages, and much more surrounding badges.

Badge Books are what is best for kids and I am excited for all of the ways the Badge Books will continue evolving in our district!

It is important to note that we purposely eliminated the 1, 2, 3, 4 grading system. The concepts of beginning, emerging, proficient and mastery are replaced with simple criteria specific to each badge. A student meets the criteria or not, there is no teacher subjectivity. As they earn the badges, they progress in the continuum of learning for each standard. We have also created enrichment badges to challenge and inspire students to pursue subjects and skills about which they are passionate. The books still generate actionable data for teachers and administrators and we can continue to personalize instruction.

APPLICATION OF KNOWLEDGE

One's intelligence should not be determined on one's ability to regurgitate facts. Testing content solely to see if children can remember *stuff* does not serve children well. A better assessment would ask children to apply the concepts that were taught to answer a question or solve a problem. We need to move toward application of knowledge assessments (AKA). This is not a new idea, the Programme for International Student Assessment (PISA) has been around for decades. The difference is adopting this kind of assessment as an end of unit exam or project. When we created our integrated curriculum it was important to provide students a choice in how they demonstrated what they learned. Ultimately, we created the AKA's, see description below.

The Application of Knowledge Assessment
by Leigh Shaw, Instructional Leader

I often wonder why a concept, fact or skill is taught when the only thing happening at the end of the lesson is the teacher checking off a metaphorical box that says the students know the concept, then they move on to the next unit. Why plan a unit of study without a way for students to use it and, even better, enjoy it? The application of knowledge assessment says it all in the name itself - apply knowledge. The mere fact that students will have a choice in how they use the information and skills they are taught is inherently a motivator and tool for empowerment.

The application of knowledge assessment functions at the most effective level if it is tied to an essential question guiding the unity of study *and* students know what a possible final project is from the start of the warning. I say *possible* final project because students can always shape it themselves if they have a better idea. If planned this way, students can begin to connect and forge neural pathways as the unit builds, leading to depth of understanding.

As students develop the skills and learn the content and concepts, transferring information based on the essential question, they can begin to shape how they will wrap it all together through an application of knowledge. We do not teach for students to know, we teach for them to understand. We want that understanding to be flexible, fluid and applied to new schemas as life continues beyond a school year. We hope to cultivate students who can offer insight and innovate in new ways. Use the QR code to the right to watch our video on AKAs.

Deliberate Practice

Grades. We need to examine how and why we give grades on assignments. What does a number grade of 90 on a social studies exam tell a student? Aside from getting 10 points off, what feedback or information does the student receive that can help them grow and practice what they didn't understand? Assessments need to provide students with actionable data to actively work on items they don't understand with the goal of improving in that specific area.

Assessment should move toward the adoption of a growth mindset philosophy known as deliberate practice.

In his 2016 TED talk, *How to Get Better at the Things You Care About*, Eduardo Briceño describes the concept of the learning zone and the performance zone along with the role of feedback and practice. The learning zone is the place where you make mistakes and get better at things while the performance zone is where you apply what you have learned. Briceño believes that the predominance of time should be spent in the learning zone, but it often is not. To make effective use of our time, we need to develop the concept of deliberate practice. Briceño describes the practices of Demosthenes, an ancient Greek orator and lawyer. In addition to studying the great works, he deliberately practiced his diction by speaking with stones in his mouth, he suspended a sword from the ceiling to practice not lifting his shoulder, a bad habit he eventually remedied and, he gave speeches at the seashore to project his voice over the waves. These examples were deliberate practice at very specific skills, all of which, in addition to traditional studies, made Demosthenes a better orator and lawyer.

The concept of deliberate practice is a component of growth mindset that can be used by educators to help students overcome deficiencies in specific skill areas. In order to grow neurons, thereby growing your brain capacity, you must create assessments that give specific data on deficient areas for students. Once these areas are determined, students and teachers co-create a plan on how to remedy the deficiency.

Watch our video on Deliberate Practice through the QR code below. The diagram in the video demonstrates deliberate practice in the classroom. The outer circle represents the steps a student would take to improve in a specific area. Simultaneously, the inner teacher circle works closely with the student step by step. Similar to the two person hand car described in chapter 6, a symbiotic relationship is formed. Deliberate practice requires the student to take ownership of their learning and the teacher to provide specific feedback that is actionable for the student.

Student Agency and Ownership of Learning

"If you aim at nothing, you will hit it every time." –Zig Ziglar

How often do we ask our students to set goals? If we do ask them to set goals, how often do we hold them accountable for working toward them? We fool ourselves when we believe that report cards and earning good grades somehow serve as tacit goal setting. In practice, the lack of emphasis we place on goal setting leads to disengagement and a student sense of helplessness when they fall behind. This is particularly true when students do not have choice in how they demonstrate what they know.

A lot has been written on student agency. I like the way Katie Martin summarizes it:

> Agency is by definition the power to act, but this doesn't have to be misconstrued as a free for all. We all operate within constraints but we don't have to all do things the same way to reach the intended learning targets and goals. Educators have certain expectations they are accountable for teaching and there is a variety of content and skills that we want students to learn. Within the content, there can still be opportunities for learners to have choice and to drive their own learning process based on shared goals and expectations. (Martin, 2020)

Student agency is a shared responsibility. It is imperative that teachers foster and cultivate student agency. The extent to which student agency will flourish is also controlled by the teacher, since it requires teachers to release control of curriculum, structure and assessment. In a broad sense, the greater the choice and voice afforded the student, the more agency will grow.

When done correctly, a shift of ownership and responsibility transfers from the teacher to the student. Consider this scenario: a student and teacher confer to discuss goals. The teacher has standardized test data as well as student work and a discussion ensues about what the student is doing well and areas of concern. The conversation also includes a discussion about likes and dislikes, aptitudes and abilities, passions and aspirations. In collaboration, the teacher

99

and student outline goals and a mutually agreed upon learning plan that specifies the content covered, the rigor of the work and how the student will demonstrate understanding. This process does not excuse the student from performing well on the next exam (standardized or classroom). It neither waters down the curriculum nor lowers the standards. Instead, it provides the student with a choice in how and what they learn within the context of acceptable parameters. It places a lot of responsibility on the student and begins to shift the ownership of learning.

This is a difficult concept for many teachers to accept. I do not believe it is about power or authority. I believe it is more about organization and structure to actualize the process. Luckily, technology is making the process easier and easier to accomplish.

CULTIVATING DELIBERATE PRACTICE IN OUR CLASSROOM
BY STACI DURIN & HEATHER HAZEN, SIXTH GRADE CO-TEACHERS

Words we often hear from students: "I will practice more... I will practice harder... I will practice longer... Practice makes perfect."

What does practicing more, harder, and longer even look like? What if we are practicing the wrong thing? Are we really aiming for perfection or are we trying to accomplish our personal best? Many students and adults struggle with the concept of practice and how to actualize the skill.

The concept of deliberate practice was introduced gradually to our sixth grade math class to help them understand the difference between practice and being deliberate about practice. Deliberate practice is practicing with a purpose, not mindless repetition of the same thing over and over. Practice requires purposeful and focused attention to the goals one sets for oneself. How do our students get better at deliberate practice? They practice it deliberately of course! This is a skill that needs to be explained, taught and practiced. We utilized Khan Academy as a tool to help design, keep track, and work towards students' goals. We combined the concepts of deliberate practice and student agency to encourage and foster a growth mindset in all of our learners.

Khan Academy is a great tool for math differentiation. This website allowed the students to work at their current level in the curriculum, challenge themselves, reteach themselves and reinforce skills. Our students were given assignments relevant to the sixth grade curriculum each week in addition to creating their own goal. Students chose their personal goal for the week. Some chose specific assignments and others chose skills from fourth through eighth grade. Since we were in a co-taught classroom, the range varied and we spent a lot of time celebrating this.

We started out the year with a goal sheet for Khan Academy. Our Khan homework was generally our only homework for math and required students to manage their time. Students set a goal for the week and practiced the skill for 60 minutes from Friday to Friday for homework. We provided time management sheets and worked individually with students who were having difficulty managing their time, or who were waiting until the end of the week to complete their minutes.

Khan Academy allowed students to work on specific skills over and over again while answering different questions. They gradually showed progress towards a goal to reach proficiency in each individual skill, then strand. They could then choose to master a skill or strand. Along the way, when students were stuck, they could view step-by-step hints and watch video tutorials. Looking for ways to improve performance was the key to deliberate practice. When faced with a challenge or when they got stuck, we asked our students what their next step would be, then helped them learn how to find different strategies to overcome the obstacle. We also added daily Edupuzzle videos and notes that went along with the math work that was assigned. We encouraged students to keep a Khan notebook to write out some of the hints for the skill they were working on and take notes from the videos. The notes could then be used as a reference tool when they got the next set of problems.

Use the QR code to see more on Deliberate Practice.

Our daily routine encouraged a growth mindset. The class culture evolved and shifted from just doing the minutes to practicing deliberately and demonstrating productive minutes. This type of practice helped foster a growth mindset in our students, believing they had the ability to change with hard work and effort. Each morning we checked Khan and they completed a goal sheet. We had a daily discussion about progress and struggles. It was interesting to see the difference in students as they caught on and began to share not only achievements but their struggles. Some students volunteered to give others strategies and help guide them. We spent time modeling that teaching a skill showed you were a master at that skill and students learned to teach and model rather than give answers to friends. We allowed a few minutes each day in class for students to ask us or peers for strategies and suggestions. Students shared notes and utilized class notes.

As the year went on, the minutes began to increase to help build the stamina of our students. The goal sheets held the students accountable for all of their learning and meeting their goals. Students were honest. They may have stated they did nothing, others were very specific about the strategies they used. We continually stressed that they were the owners of their learning. If their goals were not being met, what did they do about it? For some students just achieving the minutes each week was a goal, which meant their homework was done. Other students accepted the challenge of teaching themselves new math that was beyond the sixth grade curriculum. As the year progressed and we added new challenges to the Khan assignments, the students grew and met new goals.

Most of the students truly learned that through deliberate practice they could actually teach themselves new math they had never seen before. Adyson was an example of a solid math student. Before sixth grade, math usually came easily to her. When presented with Khan challenges at the beginning of the year, she would often give up right away. She was not challenged in the past and did not feel comfortable making mistakes and having to put in effort. When asked what she had learned that year in math, she stated "Deliberate practice requires you to be focused, learn from your mistakes, notice what you are improving on and what you are not good at and then find new strategies to fix it." Some students were not there yet in their learning and understanding of how deliberate practice was beneficial. Some students continued to just get their minutes done without achieving set goals. However, those students did benefit from the conversations, modeling, and understanding that struggles and deliberate practice equaled learning.

Deliberate practice requires stamina and accepting feedback to achieve and it's important for our students to know things do not always come easy. They need to be deliberately taught that practice does not equal perfect, but it does equal progress towards a goal. Experiencing frustration and learning what to do about it achieves more than getting a good grade on a test. Individual growth and progress needs to be recognized. By using goal sheets and actually teaching about deliberate practice students can see their individual growth. Learning from mistakes and learning what productivity looks like is a life skill. As their mentors, this requires structure and effort from us as we guide students in their own learning path. Even our struggling math students learned to enjoy math because we were meeting them where they were. By setting goals they were feeling a sense of accomplishment and seeing success.

Digital Portfolios

When I started teaching in 1987, I remember reading an article that said the State of Vermont was going to adopt work portfolios in addition to exams as the method to assess student performance. I thought to myself, what an exciting time to be a teacher! I wish portfolios were available to me when I was a student. I still have the same wish all these years later.

Students need a vehicle to demonstrate their best work, whatever that might be. Digital portfolios provide that vehicle and allow students to showcase multimedia files such as videos, images, audio and web-based content. A typical college application includes a transcript, a brag sheet, and teacher recommendations, all of which are flat. Digital portfolios make a student come alive and literally jump off the page. Portfolios aren't limited to college admissions. They provide high school graduates with a digital resume that could be invaluable in a job search. Very simply put, students are currently judged on test scores and grades that may or may not reflect who they are. Portfolios allow students agency in how they present themselves.

Portfolios, by design, encourage varied sources of student work and performance. Districts have the ability to mandate certain measures are included while others are decided by the student. The ability to organize multiple measures allows for a broader picture of student ability, passion, and performance. In addition, districts can showcase soft skills that may appear in its Portrait of a Graduate but may not be directly assessed.

In the past, managing paper copies of student portfolios made the process cumbersome and unyielding. Those obstacles no longer exist, in fact the ability to collate, organize, and publish is easier than ever before.

Actualizing The Shift

The underlying concept of all seven of these areas is that they are embedded with student choice. We cannot underestimate the value of choice in all of the assessment options for children. Whether it be the order in which they obtain content level badges, a choice in how they present their application of knowledge, or a choice in what method they choose to accomplish deliberate practice by providing choice you're helping the notion of student agency and more practical accomplishment in their goals.

It is equally important to understand that any of the old methods can be used in a digital portfolio. I'm not advocating a revolution of assessment. I'm advocating a shift in the methodology and thinking in how we assess children to a more encompassing method using the technology and digital tools available to us. As we leverage all of our post COVID technology, it is imperative we not lose all of the good practices we've learned and implemented in our new digital teaching.

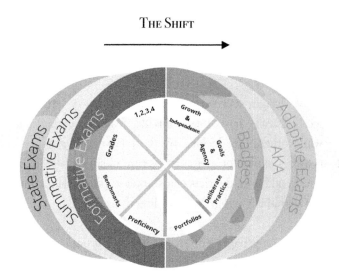

Chapter 8
Starbucks Classroom

"Build it and they will come."
- Diane Nodell, School Media Specialist
Hampton Street Pre-K School

The most critical aspect to fostering creativity, collaboration, critical thinking and communication is to create spaces where these skills can be explored, supported and encouraged. While the ideal is to structure every classroom as a flexible learning environment this isn't practical and is often cost prohibitive. Therefore, it is imperative to re-imagine existing spaces and promote the opportunity for *every* student to cycle through these spaces such as libraries, wood shops, and STEM labs.

The Learning Space Matters
by P. Erik Gunderson (2019)
Former Superintendent, Passak Valley, New Jersey

How does a learning space influence collaboration, communication, creativity and critical thinking, otherwise known as the 4 Cs? Businesses and corporations spend millions of dollars developing spaces to achieve their goals and missions. Starbucks has become popular among consumers, not by being the highest priced purveyor of coffee and snacks, but by creating a space where people have an experience that promotes communication and collaboration. Companies such as Google and Apple have created both work and retail spaces that cause employees and customers alike to become more collaborative and creative.

If private industries recognize the influence that physical space has on fostering the 4 Cs, why haven't schools invested in redesigning their spaces to enhance collaboration, communication, creativity and critical thinking within classrooms? As highlighted in chapter 1, Mike Nagler points out that the 4 Cs are some of the most important skills that students must develop to succeed. It is critical that educators do what is necessary to develop these skills to prepare our students for the future world of work!

Some districts have the good fortune of designing new educational buildings from scratch. Large, well-lit, open, flexible learning spaces that allow educators and students to construct spaces that work for their particular disciplines and needs are often highlighted on educational tours, and in educationally based architectural magazines, but the vast majority of schools are not in a financial position to tear down schools and redesign spaces from scratch.

Therefore, teachers, school boards, and educational leaders who recognize the important link between physical space and the 4 Cs are limited to redesigning or renovating their existing learning spaces to enhance motivation and enthusiasm levels for those who use that space. Creating such a systemic change to a school building becomes expensive and decision makers will often be asked to produce examples or evidence that redesigning or renovating learning spaces will benefit students.

When engaging others in a conversation about learning spaces it is imperative to focus the process on the learner, not the instructor! Learning spaces must provide students with active learning opportunities, authentic tasks, problem solving and higher order thinking skills that would help educators address the needs of the 21st century learner.

Hobson, Simms, and Knezek illustrate some of the key differences in learning that takes place in traditional versus new learning environments. The following table below lists key elements that must be considered when redesigning the learning space.

Traditional Learning vs. New Learning Environments

Traditional Learning Environments:	New Learning Environments:
Teacher-centered learning	Student-centered learning
Single sense stimulation	Multi-sensory stimulation
Single path progression in learning	Multiple path progression in learning
Single media	Multimedia
Isolated work	Collaborative work
Teacher information delivery	Student-centered learning
Passive learning	Information exchange
Factual, knowledge-based, literal thinking	Activity / exploratory / inquiry learning
Reactive response	Proactive / planned action
Isolated, artificial context	Authentic, real-world context

(Hopson, Simms, & Knezek, 2002)

Redesigned, flexible learning spaces must be more than renovated spaces that support new technologies and promote student-centered collaboration. There is evidence to show that modern learning spaces must address the need for learning to not just take place in the classroom, but allow students to network with connected students, experts, and environments outside of the classroom, thus fostering a greater sense of relevance and community (Kiefer, 2012).

Intentional or not, the form, functionality, and finish of a space reflects the culture, needs, and priorities of the people who occupy that classroom. Just as people are willing to pay a premium at restaurants and hotels for the experience of being in a particularly inspiring environment, students benefit educationally when immersed in a redesigned classroom meant to enhance engagement through the 4 Cs.

The World Economic Forum has indicated that the highest rated driver of change in the workforce is the fluidity of the work environment, specifically the flexibility of those work environments that promote co-working, innovative thinking, and collaboration. The current impact of work environment as a driver of change, along with the same report indicating that four out of the five top skills needed for future workers are the 4 Cs, suggests that there is a legitimate educational need to create space that enhances the ability for students to acquire the learning and innovations skills needed in the future global workforce (World Economic Forum, 2016).

I conducted a study at Mineola High School, in part, to determine the major characteristics and features of redesigned spaces that foster the skill development of the 4 Cs. Seventeen teachers participated in the study and three specific features were found to be of utmost importance to learners.

The first is the flexibility of furniture. Specifically, teachers indicated this was the single-most influential feature of the redesigned classroom. The efficient ability to pull tables together or apart, clear an entire floor to create an open space, and rearrange student learning centers depending upon the unit of study, were seen as beneficial and something that was not able to be replicated easily in a traditional classroom.

The second was writable surfaces. Using collaborative technology tools such as Google Drive are wonderful methods of promoting collaboration and communication from a distance, but in a classroom environment, teachers highlighted the value of writable desk surfaces for promoting collaboration and critical thinking. Four or more students could gather around a table, document a brainstorming session, solve a math problem, tilt the surface of the table from horizontal to vertical and share their thoughts and findings with the class. Teachers were also able to scan the classroom to assess progress and engagement by glancing at the writable surfaces.

The third feature was student seating autonomy. A learner's ability to make their own choices with where and how they learn, is a key element in the redesigned classroom. Teachers shared that allowing students to find alternative seating in their classrooms allowed learners to work in an environment that suited their needs. When students have the choice to work at whiteboard tables, gather at the standing-height group table, sit in the collaborative couch area, or even use one of the rocking ball-like seats during class, they feel empowered and more engaged. Each of these seating arrangements allowed for teams of students to gather and work together in a space they favored to suit their learning needs.

Although lighting, colors and other sensory features were found to be influential from a psychological standpoint, it is the flexibility, writing surfaces, and the ability to promote student choice that were deemed the most influential aspects of the classrooms that teachers believe promote student collaboration, communication, critical thinking and creativity.

In this chapter you will hear from a variety of educators, some of whom were included in the study, and their own stories about how flexible spaces, writing surfaces and autonomous learning spaces promote the acquisition of the 4 Cs. There is no set formula for the redesigned classroom, but learning from research, hearing about the experiences of colleagues and focusing on the needs of the future workplace will lead to a more engaging and motivating learning space for your students. The learning space truly does matter!

FUTURE READY LIBRARIES

A logical place to start a space transformation is the school library. It is typically the center of a building and is frequently visited by classes, learners, and the public. As well, technology has changed the traditional mindset of libraries. To keep them relevant to learners, changes are necessary to both the purpose and the physical structure. Librarians' roles also need to change. They are no longer purveyors of books and libraries can no longer be quiet spaces. The hub of the building needs to be the center of the action. If you want the 4 Cs you need to create the atmosphere in which they can exist and flourish. Makerspaces, design challenges, and coding games are all activities that should be happening at every level and in every library. Daine Nodell is the school media specialist (aka librarian) at Hampton Street School, pre-K-2. She epitomizes a future ready librarian. See her story below.

INTEREST BASED LEARNING RECESS
BY DIANE NODELL
SCHOOL MEDIA SPECIALIST, HAMPTON STREET PRE-K-2 SCHOOL

Interest Based Learning Recess, or IBL Recess, started with an idea from my principal, Mrs. Margarita Maravel. She was passionate about giving students the choice to work on something that was of interest to them outside of their classroom and, knowing that recess can be a challenge to some students, IBL Recess was created. Together we brainstormed how we could make this program a success and we have certainly created something special!

Two days out of the six day cycle, students from two classes have the choice to spend their recess in the library with me to work on activities of their choice. Rain or shine, no matter the weather, the library is always buzzing with student activity. IBL Recess allows the students to really be their own person and spend this time doing what interests them most. Students may enter together but quickly separate, going to the activity of their choice, not just following their friends. During this self-directed time, I've observed students become fast friends with students from other classes while participating in the same activity. Students can be found teaching one another how to figure out technology or simply helping each other clean up. IBL Recess is a well-oiled program with students being at the center of learning while having the opportunity to choose how they spend their time.

During this time students can use their imaginations to build with Legos, Keva Planks, Magnatiles or K'Nex either alone or with friends. They can continue to hone their coding skills that we've worked on during library time by using our Dash robots, Spheros, Ozobots or Code and Go Robot Mouse sets or continue to complete their Pathways in the kidOYO platform. The Osmo Learning System is a fan favorite during this time and the students have access to all games associated with this hands-on learning system. The students use our green screen area to create movies that utilize their building creations or scripts they have written together. They also use Virtual Reality goggles to visit national parks or zip line through the rainforest. Our students also enjoy creating with the 3Doodler pens and spend their time chatting with friends while creating their masterpieces. SnapCircuits allow students to either work alone or with several others to follow directions, build a circuit and solve different challenges. I never tire of seeing the pride on the students' faces upon successful completion of their circuit.

IBL Recess allows me to get to know my students on a personal level and to witness their social, emotional and educational growth. IBL Recess gives students the confidence to explore and learn something new in a safe environment. There's no limit to what students can achieve when they choose to spend their time at IBL Recess. I've watched many students who struggle in the classroom shine during their time spent with me in the library. If you come to the library during IBL Recess you will be amazed at what pre-K-2 students are capable of achieving on their own when you provide them the space and opportunity.

Use the QR code to see a video on IBL Recess.

FabLabs

I first heard the term FabLab when I visited the Elizabeth Forward School District outside of Pittsburgh, Pennsylvania. On the surface, it was a wood shop on steroids. Underneath, it was the catalyst for design thinking, prototyping and failing forward. When we moved the eighth grade to the high school, we seized the opportunity to require every eighth grader to take a full year FabLab course. Not only did it satisfy a New York State graduation requirement, it also provided us an opportunity to get learners excited to learn and demonstrate design thinking. It merges the worlds of engineering, computer science and the trades to provide learners a glimpse of future occupations and technology. The Mineola High School FabLab has had three major renovations in the last five years. The physical space expanded as we continued to merge the disciplines of computer science, robotics and making. Jillian Parrino's college essay below captures how learners, sometimes unknowingly, continually access the opportunities we provide them. I like to refer to it as - "build it and they will come."

COLLEGE ESSAY - ATTENDING CORNELL UNIVERSITY IN THE FALL
BY JILLIAN PARRINO
HIGH SCHOOL SENIOR

"I beleive October is my faerit moth becuase I love when the seone chane."
This sentence is taken from what I thought was an amazing letter I wrote and delivered to my parents at my second grade parent-teacher conference. Instead, it was a red flag that exposed my difficulty with spelling. Not too long after the conference, I was taken out of class to sit nervously through testing that identified problems with my auditory processing skills. Aside from my regular class work, my teachers sat me down in front of a computer, where I played "games" to strengthen my auditory pathways. As my training progressed, I began to experience firsthand the positive influence computers can have on learning. I recall vividly the mnemonic devices one of these games utilized to associate sounds with groupings of letters through the collection of balloons by Karloon the Clown. By spending an incredible number of hours on the computer with these games, I became exhilarated by the intellectual freedom I felt in this digitized world. This new world opened doors for me that pen and paper alone could not. I spent hours creating and designing PowerPoint presentations on any topic from my favorite television shows to museums I visited. Classmates even sought me out to design flyers and posters for them. In

113

the summer of sixth grade, an educational app company called eSpark, hired me to be one of two summer interns based on a video presentation I created.

Without realizing it, the countless hours spent engaged in my newfound passion led to dramatic improvements in my spelling. What emerged was a girl who loved to express herself in writing, especially electronically.

Never a day went by that I was not delving deeper into new forms of technology. As an eighth grader I was excited to be enrolled in a required technology course. While many of my peers perceived the course as tortuous, I saw it as an opportunity to explore a new part of myself.

Designing class projects exercised my critical thinking skills and piqued my intellectual curiosity in ways I had never experienced. Then, it hit me! I could use my passion for technology to solve the problems of the world just like engineers do every day.

Recognizing my abilities and fervor to learn, my teacher recommended the robotics club and encouraged me to join. Not only did joining this club permit me to express myself through technology but also through my writing. As a rookie freshman on the team tasked with writing and creating the manual that detailed the building process, I pushed aside my initial concerns and embraced the responsibility by focusing on the utilization of all my technology skills to document and record the team's development. Using this new perspective as a member of the upper-level team, I learned and implemented advanced software to design the team's business cards, safety brochures, and safety handbook.

Today, as the co-founder of my school's first ever all girls robotics team, I seek to be the gateway for others the same way technology was the gateway for me. The fact that I struggled with spelling did not take a toll on my confidence because I found a different means to communicate. My ravenous consumption of technology had a momentous impact on my life's journey. Recently, when I was asked to review a club poster for approval, I noticed the student had misspelled the same word I had nine years before. At that moment, I was hit with a wave of nostalgia. While the readers will never know the significance of the word believe, it will always remind me of how much I have grown. Most are surprised to learn that I, someone so technologically adept, was at one time totally incapable of spelling technologically adept. With determination, and my faithful friend technology, I am able to express myself in the language I love most: engineering.

As Erik Gunderson mentioned in his treatise at the beginning of the chapter, classroom furniture should be flexible and have a surface on which students can write. The age and size of the learner doesn't matter. Although he only studied high school classrooms, the concept of centers and flexible spaces start with our youngest learners.

A Glimpse into My Classroom
by Nicole Oddo
Kindergarten Teacher

If you walked into my kindergarten classroom five years ago during our literacy block, you would have seen children at four different tables. Each table had six identical chairs. There would be a literacy activity at each table while students were engaged in centers. Activities were somewhat engaging, but not always differentiated. Students were reading in the classroom library, but not all students were focused or engaged and it was rather noisy. I was doing my best to carry out guided reading with a small group at the back of the room. At the end of the day, I would plan four new centers to put on the tables for the next day and the cycle would continue. This sense of control was comfortable for me, but I knew that something had to change. One of our district initiatives was to increase student choice, something that intrigued me, especially with little ones. I believed this could have a huge impact on my teaching and the students' engagement.

Fast forward to the present, the glimpse into my kindergarten classroom looks very different. You can see students scattered around the room. Some students are working on writing while sitting on yoga balls, some laying on bean bags reading, while others are listening to reading on their iPads at lap desks. Some students choose to sit at tables to work on their individualized word work. The learners are focused and engaged. The volume is low. I am working with a small group at the back table uninterrupted.

This change did not happen overnight. I am a big believer that the classroom environment can translate into deeper engagement for our learners. After looking at the research, I was eager to try alternative seating in my classroom. I wanted students to be able to choose seats that helped them learn best. I also wanted students to engage in centers that encouraged learner autonomy.

I started small by trading the chairs at one of my tables for yoga balls I purchased off amazon and found at garage sales. The feedback was positive across the board so I began implementing the next puzzle piece. Little by little, I began adding new seating options for students such as scoop chairs, couches, standing desks, area rugs, bean bags, floor seats, lap desks etc. My goal was for the classroom to be a purposeful place to learn and feel like home for my students.

I invited my coach and colleagues to talk through ideas to make center time more engaging and individualized for students. I worked with my coach to identify which supplies would be needed to introduce choice centers.

I had to explain flexible seating to parents who were wondering why their five-year-old was sitting on the floor. I also had to put new expectations into place for students and change how students kept supplies. When obstacles occurred while introducing the new centers, we worked together to find solutions. This was possible with support from my coach, the district, and the principal.

I chose six activities students would engage in for word work using their individualized word lists. I added books on various levels to my classroom library that met my students' interests for independent reading. Students were also encouraged to work on various literacy apps during this time. Centers were introduced using the Gradual Release of Responsibility (GRR) model. By using GRR, students were able to work completely independently on each activity. Students built up their stamina. Rubrics were created for each activity with students. The rubric was a great visual to keep students focused and aware of expectations. Students were engaged, motivated, and working towards their identified goals. I shared what worked with my colleagues using the kidOYO platform. Others started to follow my lead and introduce choice seating.

Towards the end of each year, I reflected upon my teaching and set goals for the following year. It left me thinking about what was working, what was not working and where I could improve. I wanted to expand the opportunity for choice from just my literacy block to all areas of the school day.

Research shows that students' motivation increases when given opportunities to choose. I found the more choice I provided for students, the more connected they were to their learning. Students were engaged and took responsibility for their learning when choice was involved. Students were happy! These happy kindergarteners worked towards their goals, exceeded expectations and developed learner autonomy.

Use the QR code to find more information on Purposeful Play.

When we moved to our 1:1 iPad initiative, it became clear we didn't need computer labs any longer. We converted those spaces into STEM labs, which eventually led to outdoor classrooms for science exploration.

The Elementary STEM Classroom
by Katilyn Rouskas

My first kindergarten class each year begins with an activity titled *What is a Scientist?* I ask the students to describe a scientist, a mathematician, or an engineer. The majority of responses are always the same: drawings of male scientists with white lab coats, crazy hair, and goggles. When I reveal to them that this is not what most scientists even look like, they are stunned. It is truly incredible to see. I show them pictures of classic STEAM role models such as Grace Hopper, Jane Goodall, Elon Musk, Thomas Edison, and even young scientists such as TIME's 2020 Kid of the Year Gitanajali Rao. We then proceed to talk about how they themselves are scientists. We revisit their original illustrations and draw another picture of what a scientist looks like with their newfound knowledge. The second drawings are now of students like themselves engaging in STEAM, less the crazy hair, lab coats, and goggles.

As I began my undergraduate career, my professor for Elementary Math and Science Class, told us a statistic that has made a lasting impact on my passion about STEAM education for our elementary learners. That statistic stated that 60% of 9th graders lose interest in STEAM by the time they reach high school graduation. As educators, it is imperative for us to create a STEAM culture to help reverse this trend.

Herein lies my why: to inspire my youngest learners to be inquisitive, critical thinkers; innovators and problem solvers, who dream big and are engaged in design thinking as young as four years old. That's right, our pre-kindergarten students absolutely engage in the design thinking process and understand the science behind learning. Some students often remind me to reach into my hippocampus if I am struggling to remember where we left off last STEAM class!

If you were to step into my STEAM lab today, you would see students engaged in scientific phenomena, solving problems, asking questions, and failing. Failing in my STEAM lab is our First Attempt In Learning. I have worked with an incredible and inspirational instructional leader, Jenn Maichin, who has helped me to have a growth mindset. I embraced vulnerability and ambiguity as if it were my best friend. It was uncomfortable at first, but the growth I experienced and continue to experience is well worth it. We celebrate mistakes LOUD and PROUD in our classroom where learners are empowered to say they aren't sure and are then motivated to do something about it.

Our STEAM lab has undergone quite the transformation, evolving each year as we learn. In the beginning, the lab was more of a cookie cutter science room. I started by just teaching science. I followed a science curriculum and science standards. Don't get me wrong, I LOVE science and so did our learners, but I knew there was so much more potential for our STEAM lab. My lessons generally started with a know, want-to-know, learned (KWL) chart where I asked students what they knew about a specific science topic and we moved on through the lessons and experiments from there. There was much more to science and STEAM than KWL charts and scripted procedural experiments. I needed to create a more student centered, play-based environment where students were taking thoughtful risks and enjoying the problem solving process. I wanted them to embrace uncertainty and be okay with not knowing an answer right away.

After attending and networking at STEAM conferences, studying numerous research articles, and collaborating with my colleagues and administrators, we revamped our science curriculum to be more of a STEAM lab rather than a science lab. A key aspect that changed my perception was changing my mindset to think about STEAM as an attitude or a belief and not just a subject. It is critical for our learners to understand this as well. I learned early on that elementary students can rise and exceed any expectations you have for them, and I love setting the stage for engagement in and out of the lab. Our outdoor learning space allows our learners to engage in even more hands-on, nature learning experiences where meaningful learning moments will happen daily.

Every year I look forward to getting students even more excited and engaged in STEAM. Together we are educating and mentoring the next generation of learners and leaders. Together we are embracing the opportunities that foster vulnerability, curiosity and growth while welcoming the opportunities that lie ahead.

Use this QR code to find our about our STEAM Day.

Physical space, like any other part of a school system, must also go through DEV cycles and EnR thinking. Reimagining spaces is a necessary component to engaging 21st century learners. Every space at every grade level can be reimagined, as the stories suggest. DEV leaders promote and encourage experimentation with new spaces and ideas.

CHAPTER 9
THE NEW LANGUAGE

"Knowledge of languages is the doorway to wisdom"
- Roger Bacon

Some shocking statistics (code.org, n.d.)

- Nine in ten parents want their child to study computer science, but only one in four schools teach computer programming.
- Computing makes up 2/3 of projected new jobs in STEM.
- Computing occupations are among the highest-paying jobs for new graduates, yet fewer than 3% of college students graduate with a degree in computer science, and only 8% of STEM graduates are in computer science.
- In 22 states, computer science classes do not count toward math or science high school graduation requirements.
- Only 22% of AP Computer Science students are women. Only 13% are Black/African American or Hispanic/Latino.

These statistics, compiled by Code.org, are used during their annual computer science education week to draw awareness to the lack of attention schools give to arguably the most important discipline of the 21st century. This is not a new problem. In 1983, *A Nation at Risk: The Imperative for Educational Reform* (The National Commission on Excellence in Education, 1983) was published and issued a dire warning for the state of the American public education system. "If an unfriendly foreign power had attempted to impose on America the mediocre educational performance that exists today, we might well have viewed it as an act of war." The commission made several recommendations, one of which called for "five new basics." Such preparation included four courses in English, three in mathematics, three in science, three in social studies, and one-half credit in computer science. Two credits in foreign language were also recommended for students planning to attend college. (Park, 2004)

The inclusion of computer science as a mandatory subject for high school graduation has still not been realized. Much has been written about the alarming tone of the report, but its description of need in the area of computer science was right on the mark. The commission recognized, over 35 years ago, that a shift in technology was coming and we should prepare our future workforce appropriately. The report concludes with recommending new graduation requirements one of which was:

> The teaching of *computer science* in high school should equip graduates to: (a) understand the computer as an information, computation, and communication device; (b) use the computer in the study of the other Basics and for personal and work-related purposes; and (c) understand the world of computers, electronics, and related technologies. (The National Commission on Excellence in Education, 1983)

Sadly, not only was the recommendation not actualized, we currently have a dearth in qualified graduates (high school and college) that have the skills necessary to meet workforce demand. The lack of qualified workforce has led American companies to look overseas for a computer science workforce. One common way to find employees was through visas. The US H-1B visa is a non-immigrant visa that allows US companies to employ graduate level workers in specialty occupations that require theoretical or technical expertise in specialized fields. It is estimated that tech companies hire over 85,000 workers on H-1B visas. (Molla, 2019)

There is an obvious need for skilled computer science candidates and we recognized the issue over 35 years ago. Why is it so difficult to solve this problem? I believe the answer comes in three parts: awareness, demystifying the subject, and developing qualified teachers. Each answer creates a new question:

- What can we do to educate society about the importance of computer science?
- What exactly is computer science? Is it strictly coding?

123

- Without knowledgeable teachers how can we scale teaching the subject nationwide?

Awareness

In December 2014, President Obama became the first president to write a line of code, but, prior to 2013 the word coding wasn't a common term. The creation of the not-for-profit Code.org started to make coding a household name. Social media was inundated with videos, many featuring celebrities, about the importance of computer science. The founder of Code.org, Hadi Partovi, explains it like this,

> The idea for Code.org isn't that every kid should learn to code, it's that every school should teach computer science. We use the word 'coding' because it's more hip. But computer science really is a subject that needs to be taught. And the reason for this isn't because there's so many coding jobs or that coding pays well or things like that. The reason is because computer science is foundational. Every school teaches biology, every school teaches chemistry, every school teaches algebra. You wouldn't envision going to a school that just said, 'We don't teach that.' I believe schools should be mandated to teach computer science. You would never send your child to a school that didn't teach math. In the 21st century, computer science is as important as biology. Understanding photosynthesis or H2O or electricity is just as foundational as understanding how the internet works or what an algorithm is. These things are impacting our daily lives. We need future lawyers and doctors and politicians to all understand it. We're not trying to prepare kids for jobs. We're trying to prepare kids for life. (Gelles, 2019)

Demystification

What exactly is computer science? In order to make the subject more tangible, it is beneficial to identify components of the subject we want to teach students and also enable educators to craft curricula needs and teaching responsibilities. Let's start with some definitions:

- **Coding** is the practice of developing a set of instructions that a computer can understand and execute.
- **Computer science** is "the study of computers and algorithmic processes, including their principles, their hardware and software designs, their applications, and their impact on society.
- **Computational thinking** is "a way of solving problems, designing systems, and understanding human behavior that draws on concepts fundamental to computer science... a fundamental skill for everyone, not just computer scientists."

Defined this way, coding can be considered a technical skill, computer science is an academic discipline, and computational thinking is a problem-solving process central to computer science that can be applied more broadly to problem solving and learning in any discipline. (2022)

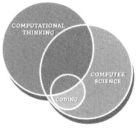

(Mills et. Al., 2021)

WHERE ARE THE TEACHERS?

There aren't enough teachers that are certified or knowledgeable enough to teach computer science. "In 2016, only 75 CS teachers graduated from pre-service preparation programs. (In comparison, nearly 10,000 Math teachers graduated that year–and another 12,000 Science teachers)." (Bigman, 2019) In fact, most states don't even have a certification in the subject. If we wait until states and colleges develop certification programs we will continue to delay implementation. That is of course assuming students want to become teachers, prospective candidates will surely be lured into private industry that will provide much more lucrative salaries and benefits. I believe the answer lies in developing partnerships with outside vendors to supply the expertise that is needed.

Mineola's Journey

In February 2013, Board of Education President, Christine Napolitano, sent me an email with a link to a video of will.i.am speaking about the importance of learning to code. Her message was simply, "What are we doing about this?" That prompted me to educate myself about computer science and coding. On March 2, 2013, I wrote a blog post entitled *Should every student learn how to code?* My thought process at the time was traditional - in order to make room for a new topic an old topic needed to be eliminated or changed. Of course, when you suggest this type of change, people tend to dig in their heels about the past. This is NOT an example of EnR thinking. While no one refuted the importance of the subject, there certainly was consternation about the proper way to implement it.

A Shift Towards Tech
by Christine Napolitano
Mineola Board of Education Trustee 2009-2021, President 2016-2021

I'm not an educator, but I had the unique opportunity to join the Board of Education when Dr. Nagler took the helm. Fortunately, I had already known him for years, so I felt comfortable enough to bounce many ideas around with him. We had countless conversations about improving the educational process in our district, but the "how" was key. In looking back, it was that ease in those discussions that propelled me to send him an article about coding. Quite frankly, I had no idea what it meant to code, but I knew it was important. A friend of mine had sent it to me (her son was working for Facebook at the time). I could feel the ground shifting under us as more of our discussions pointed towards technology. I was not afraid of technology for our students (although many parents were at the time). I knew it would become an increasingly important part of our students' lives. I read countless articles and books about how the world was changing for the current and future workforce. Ignoring technology was simply not a choice. Could coding become the building block of a computer science program?

I didn't know it at the time, but for Mineola it was the start of big change and a shift towards tech and the culture of the district.

I believe we are a district where creativity and failing forward are celebrated. It has been a gradual change, and not always easy, but oh so powerful. As the vision started to crystallize, I believe that more and more people became comfortable sharing new initiatives without fear of criticism. The momentum grew and continues to flourish.

Cultivating the culture has paid off in ways I never could have imagined. Shared vision, not only amongst the leaders and staff in our buildings, but of the community is something I wish all districts could experience. It is very difficult work, but it can be done. Leadership, creativity, trust and time. It works.

The challenge became how to design a comprehensive implementation of computer science, embedded in the curriculum, without eliminating other courses. Finding the answer to this question led me on a quest to understand coding through the eyes of a student. I recruited my son James, age nine at the time, to take this journey with me. My wife registered us to take a free coding class at a local university. I really had no idea what to expect, but I do remember we had to create an account on a platform called OYOclass and then download something called Javabeans - I was generally confused. When we arrived, James was immediately immersed in a Java coding project and a light came on in my head. After the class, I approached the instructor and asked if their program was in any local public schools. His reply was, "The schools don't want to speak to us." I replied, "You're speaking to one now." A few meetings later, a partnership was born.

kidOYO

Devon and Melora LoFretto launched kidOYO in 2006, soon after their son was born. They describe the platform as an "educational initiative to test the earliest ages at which kids could engage a meaningful real world entrepreneurial learning process driven by the development of skills that were rarely accessible in school-based classrooms. Our early software + manuscript set out a philosophy of kids 'owning your own' learning, including the pace, interest-based progression, tools, identity, and data associated with that learning." (Searls, 2019)

I describe the platform as a one stop shop that allows students to explore all aspects and difficulties associated with computer science. The web-based program organizes content in courses or small, discrete learning in a coding language. Once a student finishes a course they take a challenge to demonstrate mastery of the content learned. If they are successful, the student earns a badge. The beauty of the platform is that it can be fully independent of school. The challenges are graded virtually and the courses are created by content experts, which solves the problems of finding and hiring certified computer science teachers.

Simply purchasing the OYOclass platform is hardly a partnership. We wanted to embed coding in content classes and begin to train teachers on basic coding skills and computational thinking to help facilitate scaling CS K-12. We began by creating committees, by grade and by discipline. For more on kidOYO use this QR code.

COMPUTER SCIENCE, CODING, ROBOTICS AND MAKERSPACE COMMITTEE
BY DR. NICOLE CULELLA
INSTRUCTIONAL LEADER

How does a district establish, cultivate and maintain an inclusive group of stakeholders (educators, students and community members) to implement new and innovative Computer Science/Coding/Robotics/Makerspace technology? More critically, how do we instill the value and importance of those technologies and why is having a foundational knowledge of them essential for every student?

In September of 2017, Dr. Nagler assigned me the following tasks:
- Establish a learning continuum for coding languages pre-K-12
- Embed computer science and coding into subject classes
- Establish a learning continuum for makerspaces and robotics pre-K-12
- Create and scale our own acronym for a design thinking process

He didn't give me any specific directions, he merely said we need these things done, figure it out.

My decision was to create a districtwide committee, representing all grades and schools comprising key stakeholders that were passionate about STEAM, had demonstrated seeds of creativity and innovative thinking or were simply members of their school community and potential advocates for experimenting with and replicating innovation. Simply stated - we found our champions.

Coming to the educational field with a civil/structural/biomedical engineering background, I know how the cross-pollination of discrete disciplines and fields results in the formation of both innovation and future-ready individuals. What was needed in our organization was the same thinking that I was indoctrinated with in engineering school, we teach you how to think. The technology, software, and applications taught might become obsolete and dated over time, but the process of engineering design thinking (the design process) will remain the cornerstone of iteration and innovation. When individuals are equipped with this approach to learning, they are able to flexibly adapt as well as continue advancing any field of study. My challenge: How might I be able to have district key stakeholders not only understand but promote this process of thinking in all of our learners?

The committee began with a fundamental shift in thinking- we are not conveyors of information, but facilitators cultivating students to learn. how to think. Alvin Toffler put it like this, "The illiterate of the 21st century will not be those who cannot read and write, but those who cannot learn, unlearn, and relearn." That was the basis of design the committee used in creating pathways and curriculum. This fundamental shift from what students know and understand to how students think was critical. In Mineola, putting emphasis on the process of thinking and learning has become the norm. Dr. Nagler has been an avid supporter of this work by creating both the culture and environment that allows others to articulate, develop and sustain the district's vision into reality.

The committee was an anchor in calling out the design thinking process as the fundamental piece in redesigning curriculum and professional development experiences pre-K-12. The committee uncovered the natural interconnectedness of the design thinking process with educational theories and practices they have previously encountered in their professional careers. Bloom's Taxonomy, Webb's Depth of Knowledge, Costa's and Kallick's Habits of Mind, Dweck's Growth Mindset and Hattie's Mindframes for Visible Learning all fit into what we were striving to accomplish with computer science, coding, robotics, and makerspaces. The takeaways from all of these works synthesize sound teaching and learning practices.

The committee used the design thinking process to brainstorm how the district could create a progression for coding languages and more importantly provide learners the opportunity to use these languages in their content classes. The committee also wanted to visually represent this work in easy to understand formats. The diagram below demonstrates the progression of coding languages.

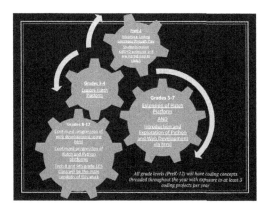

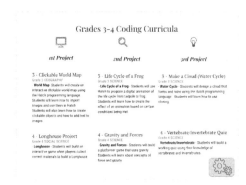

Grades 3-4 Coding Curricula

1st Project

2nd Project

3rd Project

3 - Clickable World Map
Grade 3 GEOGRAPHY
World Map - Students will create an interactive clickable world map using the Hatch programming language. Students will learn how to import images and use them in Hatch. Students will also learn how to create clickable objects and how to add text to images.

3 - Life Cycle of a Frog
Grade 3 SCIENCE
Life Cycle of a Frog - Students will use Hatch to program a digital animation of the life cycle from tadpole to frog. Students will learn how to create the effect of an animation based on certain conditions being met.

3 - Make a Cloud (Water Cycle)
Grade 3 SCIENCE
Water Cycle - Students will design a cloud that forms and rains using the Hatch programming language. Students will learn how to use cloning.

4 - Longhouse Project
Grade 4 SOCIAL SCIENCE
Longhouse - Students will build an interactive game where players collect correct materials to build a Longhouse.

4 - Gravity and Forces
Grade 4 SCIENCE
Gravity and Forces - Students will build a platformer game that uses gravity. Students will learn about concepts of force and gravity.

4 - Vertebrate/Invertebrate Quiz
Grade 4 SCIENCE
Vertebrate/Invertebrate - Students will build a working quiz using their knowledge of vertebrates and invertebrates.

The diagram to the left is an example of how we connected coding projects to curricula work. It is important to note that we realized these frameworks had to be flexible - as learners explored coding languages in the early grades, we had to evolve the curricula progression to match learner skills and interests. Our strong partnership with kidOYO made our vision that much easier to achieve.

The committee and I were also unwavering in threading and embedding coding opportunities within our makerspace movement. We wanted to develop connections between how coding and computer science influences hardware and machines. We decided to partner with For Inspiration and Recognition of Science and Technology (FIRST). Their progression of competitions was not only age appropriate but complemented our curriculum. It also provided us a clear pathway for students to follow that showcased their knowledge and understanding of coding as well as engineering fundamentals.

The committee wanted the design thinking process to become "sticky" throughout the district. They felt strongly that the process should be subject neutral and valuable to learners regardless of the problem they are tackling. It was critical to reinforce computational thinking across disciplines. Computational thinking, unlike coding, is the tool in molding students on how to think. The components of decomposition, pattern recognition, abstraction and algorithm design help our learners to develop their problem solving skill set. In order to embed the problem solving design process into our content, we further studied and brainstormed various engineering design processes. We ultimately created our own acronym using Mineola's mascot, the Mustang.

To the right is the graphic that was created from our committee work to utilize in the pre-K-2 grade levels. We purposefully created two graphics, one to use with our pre-K-2 learners and one to use with our 3-12 learners We had our learners in grades 3 and 4 transition to the more abstract graphic (to the left) by having students see and utilize both of them.

Last, we developed a way to both celebrate and promote transparency for district community stakeholders to understand the design process and the progression of skills that the districtwide committee developed and implemented. Hence, the #MineolaProud Event in our District was born. This event is not your traditional science fair or school share out. This event is organized in such a way as to have the districtwide committee work become transparent to the community at large. For example, having a room for just computer science and coding where a parent can see the progression and growth of experiences for their child from pre-K-12 was powerful and enlightening. This motivates not only the broader community members to understand the importance of the progression, but for learners and teachers in the district to finally put meaning to and grasp the concepts they might have viewed as random or isolated before. By fully experiencing the progression of skills, buy-in is further developed amongst the broader community members and the work of the districtwide committee is further realized and developed. This is where everyone in the organization is able to understand how the pieces fit together.

◇◇◇

As we launched AP Computer Science Principles for every ninth grader, we continued to think about what came next. We built dual enrollment college coursework on OYO that allowed us to offer fully asynchronous classes for students that moved quickly through our in-person classwork. While building OYO University, our discussions were focused on multiple ways, in and outside of school, that kids could choose to pursue computer science.

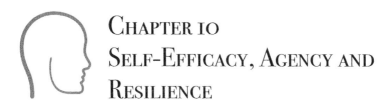

Chapter 10
Self-Efficacy, Agency and Resilience

"Learning is hard, it's supposed to be."

- Jennifer Maichin
Instructional Leader

We need to teach brain plasticity to 4-year-olds. That's not how it started, but our goal to teach learners to be more independent and advocate for themselves really took hold when we started our growth mindset initiative. The pandemic changed the title of this chapter. Originally, it was called Celebrate Mistakes, a shout out to one of the tenets of growth mindset. As our work during the pandemic heightened our emphasis on SEL, the chapter had to be more comprehensive. Our foundational work in the growth mindset allowed us to accelerate our work in SEL, but let me start at the beginning.

My growth mindset urgency began during one of my usual building tours one fall. The noise and activity wasn't what drew me to Jenn and Staci's class, it was always like that. The difference this time were the strange signs hanging around the kids' necks. Richie Hradek was wearing a Weekend Warrior sign around his neck and a huge smile on his face. He stopped me to tell me how many hours he logged on Khan Academy over the weekend and then went away. Unusual things always happened in this class. Stuffed neuron cell toys were passed around as recognition and students snapped their fingers to demonstrate they were learning and growing neurons. Perhaps the most unique aspect was the dialogue - students readily admitted they didn't understand or they were struggling to grasp a concept. No one was embarrassed to say "I don't get it." They had a firm understanding of what they didn't know.

Jennifer Maichin and Staci Durnin have been co-teaching for years. Jenn is our resident expert on growth mindset and the two teachers have perfected the concept of deliberate practice (a tenet of growth mindset) over the years. Learn more through this QR code.

Their classroom is a model that could and should be replicated everywhere and became the birthplace of the Mineola Growth Mindset initiative. The catalyst for the movement was none other than my Weekend Warrior, Richie. It started a few years prior in the seventh grade. An odd number of classes necessitated an unusual configuration in which one teacher taught all four subjects with a special education co-teacher (Jenn). The class consisted of gifted students as well as children with IEPs. Jenn affectionately called it the Think Different class, and after a dozen years of teaching, became her greatest challenge.

That class deepened Jenn's understanding and application of growth mindset and sent her on a professional journey in which she eventually partnered with MindsetWorks. At that time, MindsetWorks was the global leader in growth mindset development leveraging the pioneering research of Carol Dweck and Lisa Blackwell. While the gifted students often questioned the growth mindset (GM) beliefs, the students that struggled found new hope. One student in particular, Matteo, became the champion of the growth mindset philosophy. He was able to publicly articulate how his mistakes made him smarter and how his failure fueled his desire.

I was so impressed with what I witnessed that day that I invited Jenn, Staci, and their students to give a presentation on growth mindset during a Board of Education meeting. After the students spoke, there were not many dry eyes in the room.

The students demonstrated their belief in their capacity to grow. They articulated that true learning is effortful and includes necessary obstacles and setbacks. Learning is their choice and only they can grow the neural pathways in their brain. They taught us their mantra: Easy is boring. It was so obvious that these middle school students owned their learning and a new belief system had been ingrained in their minds, a belief that they would carry well past middle school.

That was the moment the snowball was formed and the avalanche soon followed. By the end of the school year, a plan was formed to implement a growth mindset districtwide. We partnered with Mindset Works and arranged for Eduardo Briceño to give a keynote on Superintendents' Conference Day to kick off the initiative.

We had a very talented videographer on staff that we enlisted to create a year-long documentary on our implementation, and we decided Richie would be the narrator (and the star) and so began *The Process: A Year of Growth Mindset at Mineola* (Nagler & Gavin, 2017). Use the QR code to watch the documentary.

Matteo graduated that year and his senior project involved his own journey in school and the role that growth mindset played in his life. Instead of the typical welcome back series of administrative speeches and meetings, we decided to open Superintendents' Conference Day with a TED talk from Matteo, immediately followed by Eduardo. Together they brought down the house.

The movie pre-dates the DEV cycle, but all of the components are easily visible. Teacher attitudes and preconceptions, individual epiphanies and triumphs were all on display. Eduardo's keynote focused on the concept of the learning zone and the performance zone, which really resonated with the staff. We started to see a new understanding of the role of assessments and greater emphasis on failing forward in the learning zone. The movie also depicts how we introduced teacher choice professional development and started to practice what we preached. We generated classroom resources, created videos, and celebrated mistakes. We had the beginning foundations of a movement. You can see the stages of the DEV cycle as they played out over the year.

The second year Rinse and Repeat was critical to continue painting the picture of the importance of growth mindset. How would we walk the talk? How would we send the message that this initiative was not going away, that we were all a part of the process of cultivating a growth mindset culture?

Not long ago, we opened the school year with two TED talks from Mineola High School seniors, describing the impact of teachers on their lives. Both talks spoke to the humanistic side of education - the nonacademic life lessons that occur in the learning zone. Year two began with a bang. Teachers were energized to continue the work, and we invited more people to talk about the project.

We certainly scaled the number of teacher champions and the movement was much more apparent in buildings outside the middle school. Teachers gained a new and deeper understanding of the growth mindset and the conversations in professional learning community meetings shifted. We had many bright spots throughout the district. We continued the momentum by holding a movie premiere for *The Process* that spring. Over 800 people showed up to the premiere and the high school auditorium was filled with community members and interested educators from neighboring districts. The film received rave reviews. As the second year of implementation drew to a close, from my perspective, our GM initiative appeared to be going smoothly. I ran into Jenn and asked for her reflection. She was not happy with the scale of the implementation, specifically with students. We had many conversations about the difficulty in changing adult minds, especially teachers and parents who have had fixed mindsets ingrained since they were children. We needed to make changes in the next Rinse and Repeat cycle. The logical conclusion was to intensify our efforts with our youngest learners. She felt we could and should do more, and I agreed.

One of the most important roles of a DEV leader is to empower your champions. Jennifer Maichin was an underutilized district asset who was literally was a national expert on growth mindset. I needed her to scale her work in the district, so I made her an offer she couldn't refuse.

Growth Mindset DEV Cycle
by Jennifer Maichin
Instructional Leader

Teachers want to inspire: "You can do this." "I believe in you." "Don't give up."

As a new middle school special ed teacher, 25 years ago, I felt passionate about inspiring my struggling learners. I was their cheerleader, their guide, their coach. It was rewarding, fun, and motivating. Together we worked, learned, and persevered. Each student left for the year feeling successful. When we were together, they didn't give up.

I, in turn, was inspired. These students were going to remember me and the difference I made. I was proud of the difference I believed I had made.

At the end of one year, a former student came back to me and told me they had given up on school because it was just too difficult. I didn't know what to say. *I believe in you* wasn't going to cut it.

I didn't know how to respond. Why didn't the inspiration, the support, the guidance and my *I believe in you* messages transfer to them having the self-efficacy and agency to say *I believe in ME*? What was I missing?

Here started my new cycle: I had a "problem of practice." I asked myself how I could shift my own practice from them viewing me as the inspiration for their temporary success, to empowering them to believe that they were the ones responsible for their own success?

Searching through the internet, I happened upon a book called *Mindset: The New Psychology of Success* (Dweck, 2006). Carol Dweck and Lisa Blackwell's research would change my life and, in turn, change the way I approached learning. I have not shut up about it since.

I learned that when students (or anyone) hold the belief that they are in control of growing their ability, intelligence, and skills, they not only have higher achievement and success throughout life, but they have a higher sense of agency and resiliency. They believe that the capacity for growth is within themselves. Conversely, when they believe their abilities are outside of their control, they tend to depend on or blame others for their successes or failures. They see effort as fruitless and give up easily leading to lower motivation and, therefore, lower long term achievement throughout their lives.

The best part... we have the ability to shape mindsets. Explicitly, teaching the malleability of the human brain paired with explicit praise and feedback for strategies and effort instead of the end product or results leads to self-efficacy, agency and resilience. Empowerment.

Throughout these years, I developed a relationship with Mindset Works. The organization, created by Dr. Carol Dweck and led by Dr. Lisa Blackwell and Eduardo Briceño, is dedicated to scaling the research. I became their in the field collaborator, co-creating and testing out strategies and materials that developed growth mindset in adolescents. Throughout this collaboration, I suggested that we add a simple three letter word to the language we use when we teach: yet.

Being a special education teacher, I had many opportunities to collaborate with many educators and administrators. I used these opportunities to share what I had been learning. Together, we dove deeper into the research and learned and discovered new ways to create and implement practices and strategies in our classrooms with the intent to engender growth mindsets in our learners. We learned that not only were we empowering our learners, we were becoming empowered ourselves. We were going through our own DEV cycles and we didn't even know it. What we were doing just made sense.

The administration in Mineola creates the conditions for teacher agency while focusing on the goal of innovation through iterations. Challenges are reframed as opportunities. If it's good for kids, let's try it.

When we first introduced iPads to the district, Courtney Zaleski and I were challenged to flip the classroom. We taught a group of twenty-five seventh grade volunteers who were inspired to Think Different and learn together all day long. The foundation of that class was rooted in growth mindset language and practice, it had to be. We were co-creating something that had never been done before.

A few years later, Staci Durnin and I had been working to create the conditions, instill the practices and use the language that would cultivate growth mindsets in our learners.

It was working. NOT focusing on the product or the end result, but instead intentionally focusing on the process changed the way we would forever view teaching and learning. Better yet, our students felt it and they wanted others to know, too.

Mike has already mentioned both Richie and Matteo, and the next year's focus on professional development and the resulting filming of *The Process* (Nagler & Gavin, 2017), but what he didn't relay is what happened in the next Rinse and Repeat cycle.

Though growth mindset was now a common term throughout Mineola, we noticed that, to many, it still felt like a this-too-shall-pass initiative, as is common in education. Understanding that this is part of the cycle, we asked the teachers what was working, what wasn't. This led us to the next phase in the cycle. How might we move the growth mindset from a catch phrase to a belief system in ALL of our learners? How might we strengthen the growth mindset culture throughout our community?

Setting the foundation is important: PD, guest speakers, early adopters. How would we build upon this foundation? How could we move past inspiration and into ownership and empowerment?

This led to the next interpretation of the cycle. The answer was in the language.

In Mineola we are driven and innovate in many ways to actualize our mission. The learning sciences teach us that without a growth mindset and the true belief that struggle and effort are necessary for growth, we may not believe that we are able to realize the tenets of the mission. Maybe they are great things to strive for, but they are for someone else, not me.

Knowing the neuroscience of learning, specifically the malleability of the brain and neuroplasticity, the brain's ability to wire and require neural pathways is a key component of having a growth mindset. Mike wanted to make this language tangible and meaningful. He knew that using a common language was essential for building culture. Can you teach neuroscience to 4-year-olds?

As I was about to enter my 23rd year as a teacher in Mineola, Mike offered me my dream job: become a teacher on assignment and take on the challenge of creating a Mineola learner language rooted in the neuroscience of learning, and start with the 4-year-olds. If we provide them with this foundation early, they will be the ambassadors. They will own the language and we will learn and grow from and because of them. They would teach us that learning is a process that is full of mistakes and not-there-yets and buzzes. Why? Because science says so.

We did it! Alongside the teachers and administration in the early elementary buildings we worked to figure out what stuck. "Pop, buzz, zap" was becoming our pre-K-2 learner language.

Then, there was the pandemic, but it stuck. We needed a growth mindset more than ever. Not only was our district prepared because of the innovation and design processes we had embraced before the pandemic, but we were also already speaking with a growth mindset. When things became challenging, and they did, the messages that were communicated were authentic. We could do this because we had already practiced turning challenges into opportunities. We could embrace the struggle because we knew that we would grow from it. We were learners.

A couple years later, SEL became the new catch phrase, with good reason. Everyone's social and emotional health and well being needed to be acknowledged and we, as well as our students, needed the arena and the tools to do so. As with many things in education, the term SEL remained at surface level in many places, but because of the years of work that we had already done to build the foundation and walk the talk, we were ready for our next cycle. We were already authentically integrating SEL with our language and practice.

Learner Language, SEL, and cultural responsiveness became a year-long Board goal.

Mike became our lead learner and the messaging using growth-oriented language was evident on all levels in the district. We deliberately refrained from over-using the term growth mindset because the growth-oriented language and messaging was becoming authentically embedded in the culture. It was no longer a catch phrase or a poster on the wall.

To support the systemic growth of learner language and a learner culture, we again went to the experts. Building off of our relationship with Stanford and Project for Education Research That Scales (PERTS), we developed relationships with the researchers from the University of Chicago consortium on academic research and CASEL. While learning directly from them, we provided them with examples of how we translated their research into practice so they, in turn, could learn from us.

How do we know it is time for a new cycle? How do we know we are actualizing this vision? How do we know that we are shifting from inspiration to empowerment? How do we know when we have actualized this vision?

The answers to these questions are in the beauty of embracing the very process we've been discussing and the DEV cycle mindset.

This next cycle was exciting, yet ambiguous. As the learners of our Mineola community embraced this mindset we saw an increase in responsible risk taking, which led to a sense of empowerment and greater agency. The result was agency and innovation, leading to out of the box ideas that became actualized because we were no longer striving for perfection, but progress.

Failing forward was not only a practice, but an expectation because it led to innovation and growth.

The Board of Education approved my recommendation to offer full day pre-K to every child in Mineola (this used to be a lottery). This luxury of additional time seemed the perfect opportunity to take a deep dive with growth mindset in 4-year-olds. The earlier we started the better chance we had to dispel societal beliefs that intelligence is genetic. With Jenn as the point person, we started to hone in on age appropriate, content specific lessons on the functionality of the brain for our youngest learners. An emphasis was made on teaching how the brain works as you learn new things. It's as easy as ABC.

ELENA GROWS NEURONS
BY JENNIFER MAICHIN
INSTRUCTIONAL LEADER

In September, Elena and her classmates were introduced to the parts of their brain. They used the words hippocampus, prefrontal cortex and amygdala. Most importantly, they learned about neurons. THEIR neurons. They learned that the only way to get smarter is to pop, buzz, and zap their neurons into forming new connections in their brains. They learned that their teachers and their parents can introduce them to new things and new ways of learning, but only they can grow their own neurons in their own brains. Actually getting smarter? Well, that's up to them. How do we know? Scientists say so.

It's a Friday in early October, and Mrs O'Grady is using the afternoon to individually assess students on the badges they have been working on for the last few weeks. Being only four, the experience of being formally assessed is quite new to Elena and her classmates. Often, the introduction of formal school is the beginning of a journey where students (and adults) begin to label

143

themselves into the categories of smart or not smart, comparing their progress, or lack thereof, to those around them.

Since September, Elena and her classmates have experienced that the assessment of skills in their class is merely a checkpoint on their road to mastery. If they aren't there yet, instead of a mastery badge they get a neuron sticker, reminding them that they may have to do some work. That certainly doesn't mean all of the hard work they have been doing is not making them smarter. That hard work has made connections and their neurons are certainly buzzing, but it's going to take a bit more time and effort to make a stronger connection.

It's Elena's turn and she is being assessed on her ABC badge. In order to get a mastery sticker the student must be able to articulate each letter in the alphabet in the correct order. Elena confidently begins her ABC song but blends the LMNOP, as so many little ones do. Mrs. O'Grady gives Elena a neuron sticker and congratulates her for her effort. She has been working hard to connect her neurons for her ABCs, but she isn't quite there yet. A little bit more practice and those neuron connections will certainly get stronger! All she has left is LMNOP. What progress!

Elena seems disappointed at first, then pensive. "OK," she says. The day ends and formal learning ceases for the weekend. On Monday morning, Elena rushes into class, she can barely contain herself. "Mrs. O'Grady, Mrs. O'Grady, I want to tell you my ABCs!!" Mrs. O'Grady stops and allows Elena to sing. When she gets to LMNOP, Elena pauses and very deliberately articulates each letter. Once she finishes her song, her eyes widen as they look into Mrs. O'Grady's tear filled expression. "Mrs. O'Grady, I did it. I didn't earn my badge because I wasn't there yet. So, I went home and told my mommy that I needed to practice and practice until I got it. Mrs. O'Grady, I grew my neurons! I just got smarter!"

Our learner language continues to grow and scale into every aspect of the school community. It isn't limited to classroom lessons. Our middle school makes it a focus of the building climate.

Mineola Middle School PRIDE: Embedding SEL into School Culture
by Amy Trojanowski
Middle School Principal

Our Mineola Middle School (MMS) PRIDE Committee is an ever-evolving, collective brainstorm focused on designing meaningful ways to engage learners, both adults and students alike, in social emotional learning strategies. Creating opportunities for middle school-age learners to invest in, apply and have fun while demonstrating positive character traits and embodying tenets of the mission of the school district is no small task. This group is committed to designing ways to embed these opportunities into our routine, resulting in a lasting impact on school culture. These routines make meaning of social emotional learning strategies in practical and entertaining ways for learners in our community.

One of the primary responsibilities of our PRIDE committee is to plan and facilitate the PRIDE assembly; a building-wide event taking place three times per year. Each assembly centers around a theme or skill. Originating with the 16 Habits of Mind, these intellectual behaviors coupled with our Growth Mindset initiative revealed common threads of mindfulness, resilience, reflection and gratitude.

Staged as a news broadcast, *Let's Talk PRIDE*, our guidance team writes a script organized in segments to introduce the focus skill/theme. Time is allowed to practice and apply this new strategy, highlight happenings in and around the school and celebrate achievements as they align to the mission statement. Anchored by beloved hosts such as *Jim Nasium* (our Physical Education teacher), *Walter Melon* (6th grade teacher cleverly disguised by toupee and mustache) and *Alli Teration* (Dual Language teacher who uses lots of lovely lingo) with feature segments from our *Mindful Maven* (Special Education and Yoga teacher), learners truly love seeing their teachers transform during each skit. Guest speakers are brought in to make connections between these themes and real-world opportunities to overcome obstacles, treat others with respect and grow. Raffles are conducted for eligible learners who earned a PRIDE card during the trimester, awarded when they are caught doing something good. Good embodies one of the Habits of Mind, contributing positively to our community or using the learner language.

Students are eager to get involved in assemblies as well. Representatives from sports teams share about their performance, learners share about participation in service initiatives and some even volunteer to share about their own experiences trying new strategies in front of an audience of their peers. We have even been known to sneak in surprise segments for added entertainment like a commercial advertising the unique invention of the People PowerPad aligned to our theme of ways to recharge your battery, our own version of Carpool Karaoke, with songs like "Eye of the Tiger," encouraging learners to explore times when they were jungle tigers vs. zoo tigers. Sometimes we have help from guest speaker Trevor Ragan, founder of Train Ugly and The Learner Lab, and even a teacher directed flash mob to lead by example and focus on the importance of coming together as a school community. On PRIDE days, our staff wear the designated shirts for the school year and students come decked out in school colors. Music replaces the transition bells between periods and oftentimes there is dancing down the hallways. Spirit is especially strong on these days.

Social emotional learning themes from PRIDE days do not exist in isolation. Surrounding each assembly, there is a series of classroom lessons and community building activities in which learners are given the opportunity to deliberately practice the focus skill and discuss when to use targeted strategies. Many of these reflections are turned into art installations to be displayed for the entire school community, and to serve as a reminder to continue to exhibit strength of character. In addition, capitalizing on instructional technologies, students are asked to reflect on their own learning and share on school-wide Flipgrids or compete in a Kahoot to review themes and strategies. Google classrooms are set up for each grade level to house SEL resources for students to easily access content to help them engage in their learning process.

PRIDE assemblies have become a celebration as well as a place that is an inspiration for new routines. Mindfulness Mondays at Mineola Middle School organically gained traction as an opportunity for learners to engage in movement, meditation, reflection and practices to reduce stress and prepare to take on challenging tasks. Learners even took responsible risks by sharing their own personal mindfulness journey over the loudspeaker during morning announcements.

Another mindfulness strategy introduced was journaling three good things to practice gratitude. Building on the existing routine of awarding PRIDE cards to learners, we adapted the same structure to supplement our commitment to an attitude of gratitude by creating digital MMS Gives Gratitude cards where members of the community were encouraged to shout out anyone from MMS and share why they appreciate them. In eight weeks we collected 868 responses! Gratitude cards were given to classmates, teachers, colleagues, friends, custodians, administrators, secretaries and parents. This amazing effort spread happiness and was palpable in and around the building.

Resilience Routines were introduced as a teaching and learning tool to guide learners through resources to build their resilience toolkit. They included student-led mediations, informative videos and question boards to ask them to articulate what it feels like to struggle or why they feel tough emotions when faced with a challenge. Learner responses helped to identify the emotions felt and find the language to develop our Mineola Middle School mantra: I feel, I lean in, I learn.

Feedback collected from all of the MMS learners is essential to the development and integration of social emotional learning strategies into the classroom and building culture. Our staff find value in practicing and cultivating their own SEL skills; they believe in making time for this learning. Their creative interpretations of how to engage our learners and help them internalize these practices has led to meaningful experiences and has quickly become embedded into the learning process and growth at Mineola Middle School.

◇◇◇

Mineola's self efficacy, agency and resilience initiatives have, like so many others, evolved over time. We began with a dynamic guest speaker and a desire to launch a Growth Mindset initiative. The documentary (entrepreneurial side of me) excited and engaged teachers, which led us to take a deeper dive and teach brain science to 4 and 5 year olds. That work led to more discussion about how brain science and social emotional learning can complement each other. As the work continued to scale, more voices brought new ideas through the design thinking process. The pieces of the puzzle started to merge and create a bigger image. Our current work is focused on encouraging and developing self-directed learners, an idea that encompasses all five tenets of our instructional plan. Assessment and grading, integrated curriculum, computational thinking, flexible spaces and agency are all merging together to paint a new picture for Mineola. One that is rooted in student choice, embraces asynchronous learning opportunities and places an emphasis on learners demonstrating use of transfer skills. We believe that self-directed learners will be better prepared to handle the ambiguity they will face when they graduate from high school and enter the fast pace of change in society.

APPENDIX I
EVOLUTION OF 21ST CENTURY SKILLS

Year	Organization/ Author	Premise
2002	Partnership for 21st Century Learning (P21)	Original framework. Partnership of business: bring power of tech to all aspects of teaching and learning.
2003	NCREL / Metiri group	enGauge multiple assessments, 4 skills cluster - digital age literacy, inventive thinking, effective communication, high productivity
2005	Chris Dede Neomillennial Learning Styles	Shifts in learning styles will prompt a shift to active construction of knowledge. Seeking, sieving and synthesizing rather than individually locating and absorbing information from a single source.
2007	NETS Standards (ISTE)	Established to codify and assess 6 major technology standards. In addition to expanding on 4 Cs they add research and information fluency, digital citizenship, technology operations and concepts.
2008	Digital Promise Signed into law 2008 (Bush)	Independent, bipartisan nonprofit, Digital Promise was created with the mission to accelerate innovation in education to improve opportunities to learn.
2009	Bernie Trilling Formula 3 Rs x 7 Cs= 21st CS	7 Cs - adds 3 to P21 framework Cross cultural understanding, computing, career and learning self reliance
2010	Common Core Standards	Standards define the knowledge and skills students should gain throughout their K-12 education to graduate high school prepared to succeed in entry-level careers, introductory academic college courses, and workforce training programs.
2011	Digital Promise League of Innovative Schools	Digital Promise League of Innovative Schools connects and rallies the most forward-thinking leaders of the nation's school districts.
2014	Future Ready Schools ConnectEd @ White House	Future Ready Schools® works with school and district leaders to implement student-centered learning strategies to target existing inequities; remedy disparities in in-school and out-of-school technology access; and use technology to create equitable learning opportunities for all students.
2017 - 2018	Battelle for Kids merges with EdLeader21 and P21	Portrait of a Graduate

Appendix 2
James David Barber Synopsis of Character Types

The first four presidents of the United States, conveniently, ran through this gamut of character types. (Remember, we are talking about tendencies in broad directions; no individual man exactly fits a category.) George Washington - clearly the most important president in the pantheon - established the fundamental legitimacy of an American government at a time when this was a matter of considerable question. Washington's dignity, judiciousness, his aloof air of reserve and dedication to duty, fit the passive negative or withdrawing type best. Washington did not seek innovation, he sought stability. He longed to retire to Mount Vernon, but fortunately was persuaded to stay on through a second term, in which, by rising above the political conflict between Hamilton and Jefferson and inspiring confidence in his own integrity, he gave the nation time to develop the organized means for a peaceful change.

John Adams followed, a dour New England Puritan, much given to work and worry, an inpatient and irascible man, an active negative president, a compulsive type. Adams was far more partisan than Washington; the survival of the system through his presidency demonstrated that a nation could tolerate, for a time, domination by one of its nascent political parties. As president, an angry Adams brought the United States to the brink of war with France, and presided over the new nation's first experiment in political repression: the Alien and Sedition Acts, forbidding, among other things, unlawful combinations "with intent to oppose any measure or measures of the government of the United States," (Barber, 1972) or "any false, scandalous, and malicious writing or writings against the United States, or the President of the United States, with intent to defame... or to bring them or either of them, into contempt or disrepute." (Barber)

Then came Jefferson. He too, had his troubles and failures - in the design of national defense, for example. As for his presidential character (only one element in success or failure), Jefferson was clearly active positive. A child of the enlightenment, he applied his reason to organizing connections with

152

Congress aimed at strengthening the more popular forces. A man of Catholic interest and delightful humor, Jefferson combined a clear and open vision of what the country could be with a profound political sense, expressed in his famous phrase, "every difference of opinion is not a difference of principle." (Barber, 1972)

The fourth president was James Madison, Little Jimmy, the constitutional philosopher thrown into the White House at a time of great international turmoil. Madison comes closest to the passive positive, or compliant, type; he suffered from irresolution, tried to compromise his way out, and gave in too readily to the Warhawks urging combat with Britain. The nation drifted into war and Madison wound up ineptly commanding his collection of amateur generals in the streets of Washington. General Jackson's victory at New Orleans saved the Madison administration's historical reputation, but he left the presidency with the United States close to bankruptcy and succession.

These four presidents - like all presidents - were persons trying to cope with the roles they had won by using the equipment they had built over a lifetime. The president is not some shapeless organism in a flood of the novelties, but a man with a memory in the system with a history. Like all of us, he draws on his past to shape his future. The pathetic hope that the White House would turn a Caligula into a Marcus Aurelius is as naïve as the fear that ultimate power inevitably corrupts. The problem is to understand - and to state understandably - what in the personal past foreshadows the presidential future. (Barber, 1972)

APPENDIX 3
ECHO CHAMBERS

We have become a society that almost requires you to be on one side or the other. Compromise, respect for an opposing viewpoint and actively searching for common ground seem to be vestiges of the past. Social media plays a large role in creating and maintaining this schism. If you participate on Facebook or Twitter you inevitably follow or join friend groups - people that share similar beliefs or backgrounds. You may also join or follow groups around common

	SCHOOLS					
Year	Willis	Cross	Jackson	Hampton	Meadow	District Total
1975	323	351	582	319	237	4,074
1976	0	352	638	375	344	3,941
1982	0	0	491	283	367	2,732
1988	0	0	510	276	370	2,634
1996	0	292	536	319	314	2,943
2003	398	237	412	207	198	2,885
2010	354	212	431	178	199	2,728
2021	54**	0	430	367	387	2,938

** Universal Pre-K

interests. Interest groups coalesce around a cause or belief and in many cases create echo chambers. An echo chamber occurs when a social structure actively discredits opposing viewpoints and it is policed to only allow members that hold the same viewpoint. Professor C. Thi Nguyen describes it like this:

> Suppose that I believe that the Paleo diet is the greatest diet of all time. I assemble a Facebook group called Great Health Facts! and fill it only with people who already believe that Paleo is the best diet. The fact that everybody in that group agrees with me about Paleo shouldn't increase my confidence level one bit. They're not mere copies, they actually might have reached their conclusions independently, but their agreement can be entirely explained by my method of selection. The

group's unanimity is simply an echo of my selection criterion. It's easy to forget how carefully pre-screened the members are, how epistemically groomed social media circles might be. (Nguyen, 2021)

As you continue to participate in these echo chamber groups your viewpoint continues to narrow and any opposing opinion is not tolerated. In Nguyen's example any "great health fact" that opposed the Paleo diet philosophy is discredited. For example, what would happen if a person wanted to post scientific studies that conclude that strict adherence to the Paelo diet may lead to heart disease. The post may be deleted or not allowed to be posted, but should it be allowed, it is likely the poster would be attacked or ridiculed for the action.

The echo chamber phenomenon is an example of the growing schism in society to be on one side or the other - common ground seems to have disappeared.
I would acknowledge that these people could be like minded in that they are open to learning from each other, open to sharing practice, open to pushing one another's thinking, not always as described by Nguyen.

APPENDIX 4

MINEOLA'S ENROLLMENT AND SCHOOL CLOSING TIMELINE

Mineola's enrollment has decreased over the last 45 years and, within the last 15 years, remains stagnant. Even with the addition of full day kindergarten and a full time pre-K program, we have not witnessed an increase in student enrollment.

Geographic location of students in kindergarten - Grade 5, 2010-2011

The timeline below chronicles the decision making of previous administrations and Boards of Education in regard to school closings and reopening. The common denominator in all of the decisions is the desire to maintain small neighborhood schools as the population decreased. Over the last 36 years Mineola has faced opposition and barriers in finding an efficient and palatable option for grade configuration.

1976 - Willis Avenue school closed, 323 students were rezoned into the remaining schools. The total district population was 3,941.

1982 - Cross Street school closed. A lot of controversy surrounded the decision of which school to close, Cross or Meadow. At the time, a consultant recommended closing Meadow because it had fewer classrooms (19 vs. 16). The superintendent cited the vast discrepancy in the condition of the buildings and closed Cross.

1988 – A $2,000,000 bond was passed to build a bus garage, elevators at the middle school and high school and six additional classrooms for Meadow because the building proved to be too small. Total district enrollment included half-day kindergarten. Enrollment decreased by 98 students from 1982 to 1988, yet Meadow still added six classrooms.

1994 - A $2,500,000 bond failed which was intended to reopen Cross and renovate Willis Avenue.

1995 – Monies were allocated in the budget to reopen Cross and renovate Willis. In May, the budget failed. When the budget went back out in June, Willis was removed, Cross remained and the budget passed. Total district enrollment included half-day kindergarten.

1996 - Cross reopened.

2000 - Bond passed to raze the old building on the Willis Avenue site and construct a new school.

2003 - Willis Avenue opens

Mineola District Council of PTAs

June 13, 2012

New York State Education Department
89 Washington Avenue
Albany, New York 12234

To Whom It May Concern,

Faced with the economic realities of most Long Island School Districts, Mineola realized in 2009 that building consolidation could result in streamlined, equitable instruction and services at a much lower cost to the District. If we did nothing, we would surely lose our programs. Our Superintendent then made a series of financial presentations to the community, replete with charts and graphs and extensive financial analysis. The logical deduction became obvious: we had a lot to lose by staying the same; we had a lot to gain by changing. The path of reconfiguration coalesced around the community's understanding of its imperative: change or lose programs.

The next task was daunting: which two of our seven buildings would close? The BOE requested that Dr. Nagler form a committee to decide. Leading change meant that we alter our self-image, from groups of neighborhoods organized around small community schools to one District, invested in one another's futures.

Dr. Nagler collaborated with the District Council of PTAs to assemble the Community Committee on Consolidation (CCC). This committee was comprised of 35 members including PTA leaders, community members (both with and without children currently enrolled in the District) as well as members of the faculty and staff. We, the undersigned, all PTA Presidents at the time, were members of the committee. We met with our individual units to understand what parents valued. These ideas were then brought to the table and discussed with the CCC.

The committee met once a week for eight weeks. The meetings were filled with ideas, concerns, opinions, and emotion. Dr. Nagler provided us with information we requested, including meeting with several architects, analysis of building space, bus routes, and staffing. After eight weeks, the CCC presented two options of reconfiguration at a Board of Education meeting. Discussion from the Board of Ed and community members ensued.

The suggestions made by the CCC were largely ratified by the community. The Mineola School District is just now completing the first phase of reconfiguration. In June, the second building will close,and in September all the grades will be in their new buildings and the reconfiguration will be complete. Mineola has been able to maintain our many award-winning programs for children in a reconfiguration described by many as a "true compromise."

We have achieved efficiency, and we have architected a model that will deliver an equitable education to every child in the District. The possibilities for professional development and collaboration are greater now that we have every teacher of grades 3-12 in the same buildings, respectively. And in the process, the tribes have united. Monday night, we had one group PTA installation for all six organizations; we have a grassroots organization (P.E.A.C.E., People for Excellence, Affordability, and Commitment to Education) which is dedicated to getting out the vote across the District; we Zumba on Thursdays. We are finally invested in the same vision.

Respectfully,
Mary Desiderio, Nicole Matzer, Patricia Navarra, Cindy Velez

References

Allison, J. (2021, September 30). *Creative destruction*. Big Think. Retrieved March 18, 2022, from https://bigthink.com/articles/creative-destruction/

Apstein, S. (2019, May 8). *Scouts are looking for life after baseball*. Sports Illustrated. Retrieved March 18, 2022, from https://www.si.com/mlb/2019/05/08/mlb-scouts-analytics-decline

Barber, J. D. (1972). *The presidential character: Predicting performance in the White House*. Prentice Hall.

Barnum, M. (2019, April 29). *Nearly a decade later, did the common core work?* Chalkbeat. Retrieved March 18, 2022, from http://www.chalkbeat.org/2019/4/29/21121004/nearly-a-decade-later-did-the-common-core-work-new-research-offers-clues

Bentley, K. (2021, April 21). *Can states meet the demand for computer science classes?* GovTech. Retrieved March 18, 2022, from http://www.govtech.com/education/k-12/Can-States-Meet-the-Demand-for-Computer-Science-Classes.html

Bershidsky, L. (2019, August 29). *Jack Ma Saves Us from Elon Musk's AI Dystopia*. Bloomberg.com. Retrieved March 18, 2022, from http://www.bloomberg.com/opinion/articles/2019-08-29/artificial-intelligence-jack-ma-shoots-down-elon-musk-s-dystopia.

Bigman, M. (2019, April 2). The Silver Lining of Computer Science Teacher Shortages [web log]. Retrieved March 15, 2022, from https://www.christenseninstitute.org/blog/the-silver-lining-of-computer-science-teacher-shortages/.

Brenneman, R. (2021, April 27). *Gallup student poll finds engagement in school dropping by grade level.* Education Week. Retrieved March 15, 2022, from https://www.edweek.org/leadership/gallup-student-poll-finds-engagement-in-school-dropping-by-grade-level/2016/03

Briceño, Eduardo. (2016, November). *How to Get Better at the Things You Care About* [Video]. TED Conferences. www.ted.com/talks/eduardo_briceno_how_to_get_better_at_the_things_you_care_about

Brown, B. (2015). *Daring greatly: How the courage to be vulnerable transforms the way we live, Love, parent, and lead.* Avery, an Imprint of Penguin Random House.

Cadwalladr, C. (2014, February 22). *Are the robots about to rise? Google's new director of engineering thinks so...* The Guardian. Retrieved March 18, 2022, from http://www.theguardian.com/technology/2014/feb/22/robots-google-ray-kurzweil-terminator-singularity-artificial-intelligence

Chen, D. W. (2020, March 29). *Teachers' herculean task: Moving 1.1 million children to online school (published 2020).* The New York Times. Retrieved March 18, 2022, from http://www.nytimes.com/2020/03/29/nyregion/coronavirus-new-york-schools-remote-learning.html

Collins, J. (2006). *Good to great and the social sectors: A monograph to accompany good to great.* Random House Australia.
Computational Thinking for Next Generation Science. Digital Promise. (2022, March 7). Retrieved March 15, 2022, from https://digitalpromise.org/initiative/computational-thinking/computational-thinking-for-next-generation-science/

Danielson, C., & Axtell, D. (2009). *Implementing the framework for teaching in enhancing professional practice: An Ascd action tool.* ASCD.

Daugherty, Paul, and Wilson, H. James. (2018) *Human + Machine: Reimagining Work in the Age of AI.* Harvard Business Review Press.

Dede, C. (2005, January). *Planning for neomillennial learning styles.* EDUCAUSE Review. Retrieved March 18, 2022, from https://er.educause.edu/articles/2005/1/planning-for-neomillennial-learning-styles

Desnoyer, B. (2014, March 10). *Founding fathers agreed: Funding Public Education is not a debate.* STLtoday.com. Retrieved March 18, 2022, from http://www.stltoday.com/opinion/columnists/founding-fathers-agreed-funding-public-education-is-not-a-debate/article_f05aa5b0-2fed-5c63-be1a-1b013cf49625.html

Dweck, C. S. (2006). *Mindset: The New Psychology of Success.* Ballantine Books.

Edelman, S. (2020, April 26). *Doe's $269m iPad deal for remote learning is a 'waste of money,' says lawmaker.* New York Post. Retrieved March 18, 2022, from https://nypost.com/2020/04/25/nyc-spends-269-million-on-ipads-for-students-amid-coronavirus-lockdown/

Englin, S. (2019, August 27). Two Decades of Free Agent Nation. *Medium.*

English, T. (2020, November 22). *Nanobots will be flowing through your body by 2030.* Interesting Engineering. Retrieved March 18, 2022, from https://interestingengineering.com/nanobots-will-be-flowing-through-your-body-by-2030

Ford, M. (2016). *Rise of the robots: Technology and the threat of a jobless future.* Basic Books.

Frank, M., Roehrig, P., & Pring, B. (2017). *What to do when machines do everything: How to get ahead in a world of algorithms, bots, and Big Data.* John Wiley & Sons, Inc.

Fullan, M. (2005). *Leadership and Sustainability.* Corwin Press/Ontario Principles Council.

Fullan, M., & Quinn, J. (2016). *Coherence: The right drivers in action for schools, districts, and systems*. Corwin.

Gelles, D. (2019, January 17). *Hadi Partovi was raised in a revolution. Today he teaches kids to code. (published 2019)*. The New York Times. Retrieved March 18, 2022, from http://www.nytimes.com/2019/01/17/business/hadi-partovi-code-org-corner-office.html

Goldin, I., & Kutarna, C. (2017). *Age of Discovery: Navigating the storms of our second renaissance*. Bloomsbury Business.

Grant, P., & Basye, D. (2014). *Personalized learning: A guide for engaging students with technology*. ISTE.

Guardian News and Media. (2012, December 15). *Will.i.am: 'I want to write code!'*. The Guardian. Retrieved March 18, 2022, from http://www.theguardian.com/music/2012/dec/15/will-i-am-want-to-write-code

Gundersen, P. E. (2019). *How does the High School redesigned learning space influence collaboration, communication, creativity, and critical thinking* (dissertation). Seton Hall University, South Orange, NJ.

Harris , J., & Istrate, E. (2022, April 5). *The future of work: The rise of the gig economy*. NACo. Retrieved March 18, 2022, from http://www.naco.org/featured-resources/future-work-rise-gig-economy

Herold, B. (2021, January 15). *What is personalized learning?* Education Week. Retrieved March 18, 2022, from http://www.edweek.org/technology/what-is-personalized-learning/2019/11

Hinckley, S. (2018, April 12). National Testing: What Does It Mean for a Student to Be 'Proficient. *Christian Science Monitor*. Retrieved March 15, 2022, from www.csmonitor.com/EqualEd/2018/0412/National-testing-What-does-it-mean-for-a-student-to-be-proficient.

Hopson, M. H., Simms, R. L., & Knezek, G. A. (2002). Using a technology-enriched environment to improve higher-order thinking skills. Journal of Research on Technology in Education, 34(2), 109-120.

Horn, M. B., & Staker, H. (2015). *Blended: Using disruptive innovation to improve schools.* Jossey-Bass.

Over 50 years of Moore's law. Intel. (n.d.). Retrieved March 14, 2022, from https://www.intel.com/content/www/us/en/silicon-innovations/moores-law-technology.html

It's A wonderful life (motion picture: 1946)--excerpts. (1946). [Film].

Kamenetz, A. (2018, April 29). *What 'A nation at risk' got wrong, and right, about U.S. schools.* NPR. Retrieved March 18, 2022, from https://www.npr.org/sections/ed/2018/04/29/604986823/what-a-nation-at-risk-got-wrong-and-right-about-u-s-schools

Kiefer, A. (2012). School furniture by the square foot. American School & University. Retrieved from https://www.asumag.com/furniture/school-furniture-square-foot.

Kirtman, L., & Fullan, M. (2016). *Leadership: Key competencies for whole-system change.* Solution Tree Press.

Kraemer, D. (2021, November 5). *Greta Thunberg: Who is the climate campaigner and what are her aims?* BBC News. Retrieved March 18, 2022, from http://www.bbc.com/news/world-europe-49918719

Lee, C. (2021, November 11). *Here are 20 major issues affecting schools across America.* trade. Retrieved March 18, 2022, from http://www.trade-schools.net/articles/issues-in-education

Lee, K.-F. (n.d.). *Changing the climate: Utopia, dystopia and catastrophe.* Retrieved March 18, 2022, from https://www.monash.edu/__data/assets/pdf_file/0003/1764219/utopias.pdf

Leins, C. (2019, September 11). States Boost Computer Science Education Efforts. *U.S. News & World Report*.

Liu, J. (2019, November 27). *High-paid, well-educated white collar workers will be heavily affected by AI, says New report*. CNBC. Retrieved March 18, 2022, from http://www.cnbc.com/2019/11/27/high-paid-well-educated-white-collar-jobs-heavily-affected-by-ai-new-report.html

Martin, K. (2020, August 30). 5 Ways That Teachers Are Using Breakout Rooms to Create More Learner-Centered Experiences in Distance Learning [web log]. Retrieved March 15, 2022, from https://katielmartin.com/?s=5+ways&et_pb_searchform_submit=et_search_proccess&et_pb_include_posts=yes&et_pb_include_pages=yes.

Martin, K. (2018). *Learner Centered Innovation: Spark Curiosity, ignite passion and unleash genius*. IMPress.

Martinez, S. (2019, February 11). *The Maker Movement: A learning revolution*. ISTE. Retrieved March 18, 2022, from https://www.iste.org/explore/In-the-classroom/The-maker-movement-A-learning-revolution

Metz, R. (2018, April 17). This Company Embeds Microchips in Its Employees, and They Love It. *MIT Technology Review*.

Miller, A. (2019, February 20). *3 myths of personalized learning*. Edutopia. Retrieved March 18, 2022, from http://www.edutopia.org/article/3-myths-personalized-learning

Mills, K., Coenraad, M., Ruiz, P., Burke, Q., & Weisgrau J. (2021, December). Computational thinking for an inclusive world: A resource for educators to learn and lead. Digital Promise. https://doi.org/10.51388/20.500.12265/138

Moe, M. (2020, May 18). *Dawn of the age of Digital Learning*. Medium. Retrieved March 18, 2022, from https://medium.com/gsv-ventures/dawn-of-the-age-of-digital-learning-4c4e38784226

Molla, R. (2019, February 28). *Visa approvals for tech workers are on the decline. that won't just hurt Silicon Valley.* Vox. Retrieved March 15, 2022, from https://www.vox.com/2019/2/28/18241522/trump-h1b-tech-work-jobs-overseas

Montgomery, E., & *, N. (2022, January 12). *Helpful tips for choosing the perfect social media influencer for your brand.* Three Girls Media. Retrieved March 18, 2022, from http://www.threegirlsmedia.com/2019/07/19/how-to-find-and-evaluate-social-media-influencers/

Muro, M., Whiton, J., & Maxim, R. (2022, March 9). *What jobs are affected by Ai? better-paid, better-educated workers face the most exposure.* Brookings. Retrieved March 18, 2022, from http://www.brookings.edu/research/what-jobs-are-affected-by-ai-better-paid-better-educated-workers-face-the-most-exposure/

Murray, Thomas C. (2019). *Personal & Authentic: Designing Learning Experiences That Impact a Lifetime.* IMPress.

Nagler, M. (n.d.). *Why education should be more like pizza - youtube.com.* Retrieved March 18, 2022, from https://www.youtube.com/watch?v=YnyQPfaSz3Q

National Research Council. (1999) *Testing, Teaching, and Learning: A Guide for States and School Districts.* Washington, DC: The National Academies Press.https://doi.org/10.17226/9609.

Nelson, M., Vaidhyanathan, S., Petrusich, A., Bradley, R., Kolbe, L., & Alison, J. (2003, December 12). *James David Barber and the psychological presidency.* VQR Online. Retrieved March 18, 2022, from http://www.vqronline.org/essay/james-david-barber-and-psychological-presidency
New Line Home Entertainment. (2001). *The lord of the rings: The fellowship of the ring.*

Nguyen, C. T. (2021, December 14). *The problem of living inside Echo Chambers*. The Conversation. Retrieved April 18, 2022, from https://theconversation.com/the-problem-of-living-inside-echo-chambers-110486

Nguyen, C. T. (2021, February 4). *Why it's as hard to escape an echo chamber as it is to flee a cult: Aeon Essays*. Aeon. Retrieved March 18, 2022, from https://aeon.co/essays/why-its-as-hard-to-escape-an-echo-chamber-as-it-is-to-flee-a-cult

Park, J. (2004, September). A Nation at Risk. *Education Week*. Retrieved September 10, 2015, from www.edweek.org/policy-politics/a-nation-at-risk/2004/09.

Piehler, C. (2020, May 9). *4 major types of educational leadership*. The Edvocate. Retrieved March 18, 2022, from http://www.theedadvocate.org/4-major-types-of-educational-leadership/

Piehler, C. (2020, May 9). *5 leadership styles that can transform education as we know it*. The Edvocate. Retrieved March 18, 2022, from http://www.theedadvocate.org/5-leadership-styles-that-can-transform-education-as-we-know-it/

Pink, D. H. (2001). *Free agent nation*. Grand Central Publishing.

Popkewitz, T. S., Tabachnick, R. B., & Wehlage, G. (1982). *The myth of educational reform: A study of school responses to a program of Change*. University of Wisconsin Press.

The power of Social Media Influencers in 2019: Cultural trendsetters. Mediakix. (2021, March 18). Retrieved March 18, 2022, from https://mediakix.com/blog/power-of-social-media-influencers-trendsetters/

Rajan, A. (2019, March 4). *Do Digital Echo Chambers Exist?* BBC News. Retrieved March 18, 2022, from http://www.bbc.com/news/entertainment-arts-47447633

Reedy, C. (2017, October 5). *Kurzweil claims that the singularity will happen by 2045*. Futurism. Retrieved March 18, 2022, from https://futurism.com/kurzweil-claims-that-the-singularity-will-happen-by-2045

Ries, Eric. (2017). *The Lean Startup How Today's Entrepreneurs Use Continuous Innovation to Create Radically Successful Businesses*. Currency.

Robertson, A. (2013, February 26). *Will.i.am, Mark Zuckerberg, and Chris Bosh tell America's kids to learn to code*. The Verge. Retrieved March 18, 2022, from http://www.theverge.com/2013/2/26/4032180/will-i-am-mark-zuckerberg-and-others-tell-kids-to-learn-code

Robinson, K. (2006, February). *Do Schools Kill Creativity?* [Video]. TED Conferences. https://www.ted.com/talks/sir_ken_robinson_do_schools_kill_creativity

Rothman, R. (2021, January 26). *Vt. forced to delay goal of expanding assessment system*. Education Week. Retrieved March 18, 2022, from http://www.edweek.org/ew/articles/1992/05/20/35vt.h11.html

Said, C. (2020, November 5). *Silicon Valley braces for new Trump H-1B rules that set $208,000 salary floor*. San Francisco Chronicle. Retrieved March 18, 2022, from http://www.sfchronicle.com/business/article/Silicon-Valley-braces-for-new-Trump-H-1B-rules-15695576.php

Schwab, K. (2017). *The Fourth Industrial Revolution*. Currency.

Schwab, K. (2020, April 20). *The Fourth Industrial Revolution: What It Means and how to respond*. World Economic Forum. Retrieved March 18, 2022, from http://www.weforum.org/agenda/2016/01/the-fourth-industrial-revolution-what-it-means-and-how-to-respond/

Searls, Doc. (2019). The kids take over. *Linux Journal*, pp. 100–120.

Sinek, S. (2009, September). *How great leaders inspire action* [Video]. TED Conferences. https://www.ted.com/talks/simon_sinek_how_great_leaders_inspire_action

Sony Pictures Entertainment. (2011). *Moneyball*. United States.

Spencer, J., & Juliani, A. J. (2016). *Launch: Using design thinking to boost creativity and bring out the maker in every student*. Dave Burgess Consulting, Inc.

Statistics. Code.org. (n.d.). Retrieved March 18, 2022, from https://code.org/statistics

Subramanian, C. (2016, June 30). *Alvin Toffler: What he got right - and wrong*. BBC News. Retrieved March 18, 2022, from https://www.bbc.com/news/world-us-canada-36675260

The Future of Jobs - World Economic Forum. World Economic Forum. (2016, January). Retrieved August 7, 2018, from https://www3.weforum.org/docs/WEF_Future_of_Jobs.pdf

The National Commission on Excellence in Education. (1983, April). *Nation at risk - reaganfoundation.org*. archive.org. Retrieved March 15, 2022, from https://web.archive.org/web/20201114000826/http://www2.ed.gov/pubs/NatAtRisk/title.html

Shelton, R. (1996) *Tin Cup*. United States; Regency Enterprises.

Trilling, B., & Fadel, C. (2012). *21St Century skills: Learning for life in our Times*. Jossey-Bass.

Tyack, D., & Cuban, L. (1995). *Tinkering toward Utopia: A Century of Public School Reform*. Harvard University Press.

Unconventional wisdom - AASA. (n.d.). Retrieved April 5, 2022, from https://www.aasa.org/uploadedFiles/Resources/Successful_Practices_Network/AASACaseStudy-Mineola.pdf

University of California - San Diego. (2018, May 31). *Cell-like nanorobots clear bacteria and toxins from blood*. ScienceDaily. Retrieved March 18, 2022, from http://www.sciencedaily.com/releases/2018/05/180531102807.htm

Wahl, D. C. (2020, April 29). *The three horizons of innovation and culture change*. Medium. Retrieved March 18, 2022, from https://medium.com/activate-the-future/the-three-horizons-of-innovation-and-culture-change-d9681b0e0b0f

Wolfram, S. (2016, September 17). How to Teach Computational Thinking. *Wired*, 1–36.

About the Author

Michael Nagler, Ed.D, is the Superintendent of the Mineola School District, a suburb of New York City. Mike began his career as a social studies teacher in NYC. While teaching he earned his doctorate from Columbia University and accepted an administrative position with Mineola in 1999.

He believes strongly in the district's mission to inspire students to become lifelong learners that exhibit strength of character and contribute positively to a global society. During his twenty three years with the district, he has been a big proponent of using technology to engage students in rigorous content. All five schools in Mineola have been recognized as Apple Distinguished Schools. Mineola is also a member of the League of Innovative Schools and Dr. Nagler is the Chairperson of the Advisory Board.

Mineola was one of the first schools in the state to implement a comprehensive computer science curriculum starting in kindergarten. Mineola is also at the forefront of digital student portfolios.

Dr. Nagler was the 2020 New York State Superintendent of the Year and was a Finalist for the 2020 National Superintendent of the Year.

More Books From Road to Awesome

(Via Codebreaker)

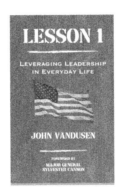

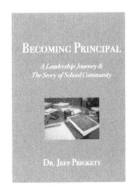

Made in the USA
Middletown, DE
04 June 2022

66578573R00106